Cookery School
Meat

Cookery School
Meat

Getting the best from your main ingredient

Joanna Farrow

NEW
HOLLAND

Contents

INTRODUCTION

Simply put, this book is designed for the inexperienced cook who likes to eat meat, as well as for those who have some experience of cooking and want a better understanding of the skills they require to become a competent cook. Learning to cook good food is both a creative and satisfying skill to master. So much of our social lives revolve around food, and cooking, eating and sharing food with others is a pleasurable experience. Making tasty food that you love to eat, whether it's a meal for one, two or a crowd is one of life's essential skills and there's no better way to nurture those you love.

If you're an absolute beginner, the trick is to begin cooking something familiar and that you enjoy eating. Plan ahead so that you have all the ingredients to hand before you begin. Ensure that you have the correct equipment, and that your cooking space is orderly and clean. Read the recipe through from start to finish to make sure you understand each process before you begin, and calculate the length of time the recipe will take to prepare and cook so that you can serve it on time without feeling rushed. Don't forget to include time for preparing and cooking any accompanying dishes, and make sure you have sufficient hob or oven space for all the dishes. Follow the recipes religiously, specifically with regard to cooking times, until you're confident enough to start adapting them to suit your own tastes. With a few successes under your belt you will relax and start to enjoy the process, as well as feel more confident in the kitchen.

This book aims to show you how to prepare delicious, interesting dishes for everyday eating without requiring the expertise or precision of a master chef. There are more than 60 tried-and-tested recipes to choose from to inspire your culinary endeavours and broaden your repertoire. Many will become time-honoured favourites that you cook again and again, while others will be special occasion treats on which you can lavish more time and attention. There's really no mystery to delicious meat cooking – all you need is an understanding of the type and quality of meat you choose and some basic knowledge of temperatures, timings and suitable cooking methods for the various cuts.

BUYING MEAT

Many factors contribute to the success of a dish, and in part, the ultimate taste of the dish will be influenced by the quality of the meat that you buy. Buying good quality meat, that is expensive for the cut that you purchase, does not guarantee the success of a meal, but if cooked properly, it will certainly add to the taste of the dish. Meat can be purchased fresh or frozen from traditional butcher shops, markets, supermarkets or farm shops. Many supermarkets also sell locally produced, native breed, premium, properly hung meats that will give you fabulous results however simply cooked. It is also possible to buy online from reputable farms and suppliers. Prices and quality vary considerably so it pays to shop around until you find produce that you like the look of. Generally the more you pay, the better the quality of the meat, but how do you know what to look for?

Our budgets often determine the types of meat we buy. It's difficult to resist meat from the supermarkets that's pre-packed and invitingly low-priced, but if that meat has little flavour then it's a false economy and a waste of your efforts. It's better to choose a cheaper cut from a well-produced animal, then cook it properly and thoroughly enjoy your supper.

Quality meat is determined by how well the animal has lived, what it has eaten, and how it has been slaughtered and hung. Breed, rearing, diet and climate all affect the flavour of meat long before it gets to the butcher. Animals that have had a natural diet, and mature as nature intended will provide tastier meat than those that are poorly or force-fed and intensively reared. Generally the longer the period of maturation, the better the flavour of the meat. Seek out a knowledgeable butcher who will be able to advise you on cuts to use for various cooking methods. You'll also be able to order ahead and buy joints that are butchered to exactly the weight you want. You're more likely to be buying locally supplied meat too.

Generally, look for meat that is neatly butchered. Chops and steaks should be of similar thickness so they cook evenly. Bone ends should look neatly sawn, not splintered, and rolled joints should be neatly tied. Don't buy cuts from which all the fat has been trimmed off since it is the fat that provides so much flavour and succulence as meat cooks. How much of the fat you actually eat is your choice.

Hanging meat

All meat needs hanging after slaughter to tenderize and to develop flavour. Even the best produced meat might be tough and lacking in flavour if not properly hanged. During hanging, whole or part carcasses are hung vertically on meat hooks in a cool environment, which allows natural chemical reactions to take place that alter the structure of the meat. At the same time moisture evaporates and the flavour becomes more concentrated. This is another reason why poorly produced meat is not hung. Its weight includes water content, which you pay for at the same price as the meat! Unfortunately for the cook who buys meat that hasn't been hung properly, this excess water is forced out as the meat is cooked, spoiling your finished dish and reducing the volume of meat served – again, a false economy.

Hanging times vary depending on the type of animal, breed and other considerations. As a very rough guide, beef and mutton should be hung for the longest, about three weeks or more. Young lamb and pork require less hanging time – about one week. Venison, and furred and feathered game are also hung to develop their flavour and tenderize the flesh, though the hanging times are more dependent on individual taste. The longer the meat hangs, the stronger and gamier the meat becomes. For many, the flavour of well-hanged birds simply becomes too strong and unpalatable but for others it's the gaminess that cuts the mustard!

Beef

Beef should be a deep dark red, sometimes almost purple, with what is known as a 'marbling' of fat running through the lean meat – these fine, thread-like traces of white fat help keep the meat moist and succulent as it cooks. Meat should not have an aged and grey palour to it. The surface fat should be creamy-coloured and both fat and flesh should look dry, not wet. Look for 'dry-aged' beef, which will have been aged naturally by hanging. Meat from cattle that have matured naturally will have a different colour to that of cattle that have been stressed.

Lamb

Sheep are seasonal breeders unlike other animals and it is this factor that inflates the price of the produce. Local lamb is only available for a short time, and the cost of importing this meat and shipping it long distances adds considerably to the purchase price, so you need to know that the cut that you buy is a quality one. Lamb should be very red, though the colour will depend more on the age of the animal. Mature lamb or mutton will be darker than spring lamb, with fat that's creamier in colour.

Pork

Pork flesh should be a rosy pink colour and the fat should look white with no wateriness. Cheap factory-farmed pork is very pale and often looks wet. This moisture will evaporate during cooking and lead to huge shrinkage of the meat so avoid it at all costs. Occasionally you might see pork, particularly steaks or chops that have a shimmery sheen that indicates that the animal has been stressed. Instead look for pork that has a rosy pink flesh and pale fat with a firm texture.

Chicken

Intensively reared chickens are fed on a diet of feed and chemicals that plump them up to full maturity in a matter of weeks and, as you would expect, results in low-quality meat. This tends to be more true of imported birds, so if you care about how your meat is raised, ask where the chicken is from and how it was matured. A slow-reared chicken fed on a diet high in natural cereals will live for at least 11 to 12 weeks and will provide you with far more flavour and goodness. It can be difficult to assess the quality of a chicken by its appearance, but as a guide choose chickens that are labelled free-range. Even within this description there are differences in the way the chickens are reared.

Duck

Wild duck are small and very lean. Usually available from a good butcher, they require careful cooking to avoid drying out. Farmed ducks are bigger, fattier and easy to cook, though intensively farmed ones will lack the flavour of good free-range, naturally fed ones. It's worth doing a bit of local research to source good suppliers. Farmers markets are a useful place to start.

CUTS OF MEAT

Butchers package meat into different cuts, many of which will be familiar to you, if only by name.
As a simple guide it helps to think of the anatomy of the animal and divide it into three main parts.
The front of the animal has the hardest working muscles and therefore the toughest cuts of meat such
as neck, shoulder and shin. These cuts are generally inexpensive, but in order to get the greatest taste
and texture from the meat, they are best cooked slowly and gently, usually using a low heat source and
often incorporating other ingredients. The central parts of the animal are the least worked areas and
include the prime, or most expensive, cuts such as fillet and loin. These can be cooked over high heat
and using a fast method. The back section of the animal has muscles that are medium hard-working
and includes cuts such as rump, leg and shank. Cooking methods for these cuts depends largely on
the animal. In most cases they're fine cooked slowly and gently, although a leg of lamb or pork leg
steaks can also be fast cooked.

Which cooking method for which cut?

Deciding on the best cooking methods for different cuts and types of meat can be a daunting process for
the novice meat cook. Cooking methods are basically either fast or slow. Roasting (with the exception of
slow roasting), frying, grilling and barbecuing are fast dry-heat cooking methods and are only suitable
for premium tender cuts of meat. Stewing, casseroling, braising, pot roasting, boiling and poaching are
slow, moist cooking methods and are suitable for the cheaper, tougher cuts. Fast cooking cuts can also
be slow cooked, but cheaper cuts will never tenderize if fast cooked.

A useful guide to suitable cooking methods for different cuts

BEEF	VEAL	LAMB	PORK
ROASTING			
rib (fore/wing)	loin	leg	leg joint
fillet	topside	loin	loin (rack)
sirloin	shoulder	rack (best end)	chump
fillet	fillet	chump	shoulder (spare rib)
FRYING			
fillet steak	escalopes (leg)	leg steaks	leg steaks
sirloin steak	loin chops	loin chops/cutlets	loin chops
rump steak	cutlets	chump chops	fillet (tenderloin)
rib eye steak	burgers	fillet (neck)	chump chops
T-bone steak	rump	burgers	burgers
burgers			escalope (leg/loin)
GRILLING AND BARBECUING			
fillet steak	escalopes (leg)	leg steaks	legs steaks
sirloin steak	loin chops	loin chops/cutlets	loin chops
rump steak	cutlets	chump chops	fillet (tenderloin)
rib eye steak	burgers	fillet (neck)	burgers
T-bone steak		butterflied leg	spare ribs
burgers		burgers	
STEWING AND CASSEROLING			
stewing steak (shin/neck)	pie veal	fillet (neck)	chump chops
braising steak (leg)	shin	chump chops	belly rashers
oxtail	shoulder	shank	leg steaks
skirt		fore (shoulder) shank	pie pork (fillet/leg/ shoulder/neck)
cheek		stewing lamb (scrag/neck)	cheek
		breast	
POT ROASTING, SLOW ROASTING AND BRAISING			
topside	leg	fillet (neck)	hock
top rump	topside	belly	belly
brisket	shin	shoulder	loin
silverside		shank	leg joint
		fore (shoulder) shank	shoulder
		breast	
BOILING AND POACHING			
brisket		fillet (neck)	leg
silverside		shoulder	hock

CUTS OF MEAT – BEEF

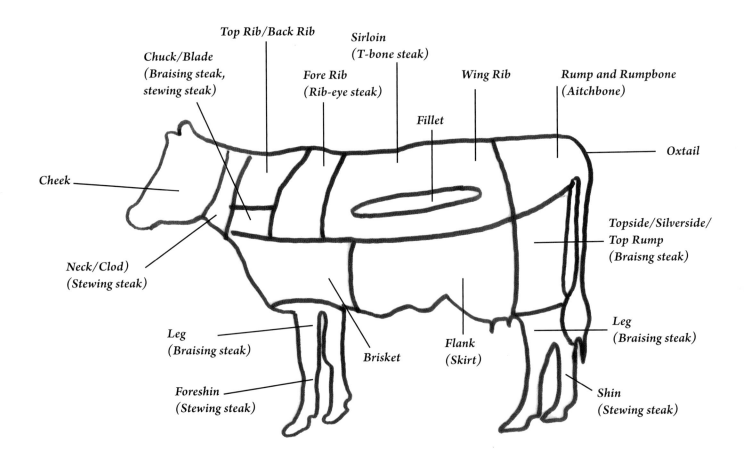

Chuck/Blade
(Braising steak,
stewing steak)

Top Rib/Back Rib

Sirloin
(T-bone steak)

Fore Rib
(Rib-eye steak)

Wing Rib

Rump and Rumpbone
(Aitchbone)

Fillet

Cheek

Oxtail

Neck/Clod)
(Stewing steak)

Topside/Silverside/
Top Rump
(Braisng steak)

Leg
(Braising steak)

Brisket

Flank
(Skirt)

Leg
(Braising steak)

Foreshin
(Stewing steak)

Shin
(Stewing steak)

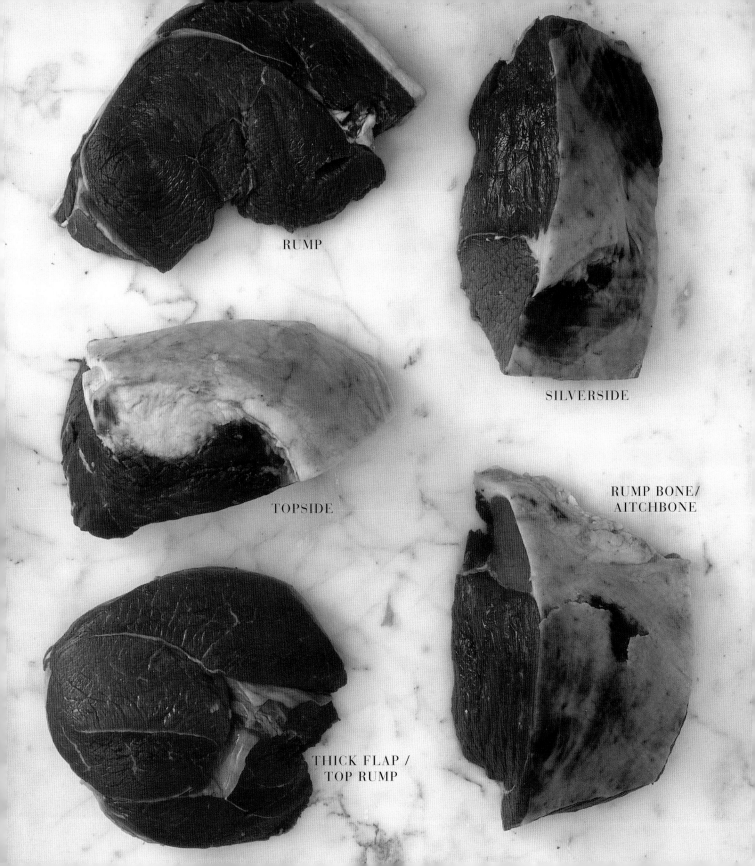

RUMP

SILVERSIDE

TOPSIDE

RUMP BONE/
AITCHBONE

THICK FLAP /
TOP RUMP

CUTS OF MEAT – LAMB

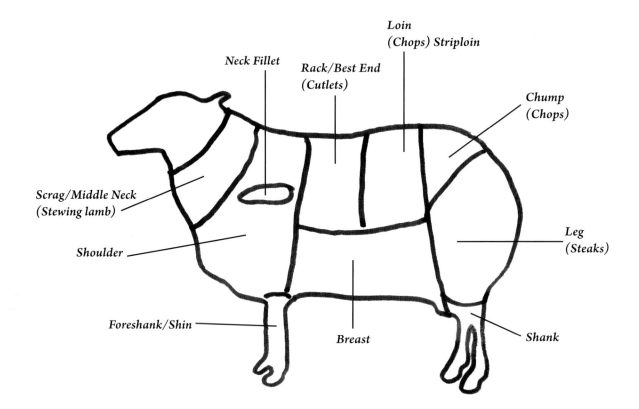

Neck Fillet

Rack/Best End
(Cutlets)

Loin
(Chops) Striploin

Chump
(Chops)

Scrag/Middle Neck
(Stewing lamb)

Shoulder

Leg
(Steaks)

Foreshank/Shin

Breast

Shank

LOIN

CHUMP

SADDLE OF RUMP

NOISETTE

STRIPLOIN

CUTS OF MEAT – PORK

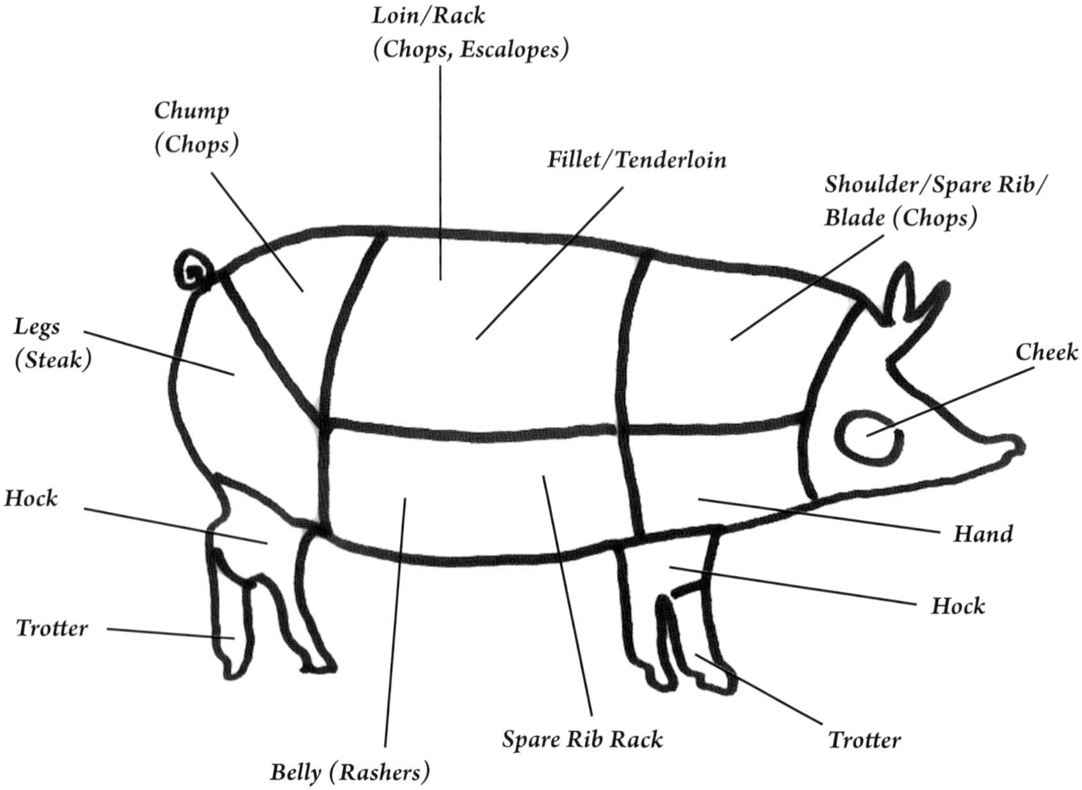

Loin/Rack
(Chops, Escalopes)

Chump
(Chops)

Fillet/Tenderloin

Shoulder/Spare Rib/
Blade (Chops)

Legs
(Steak)

Cheek

Hock

Hand

Trotter

Hock

Trotter

Spare Rib Rack

Belly (Rashers)

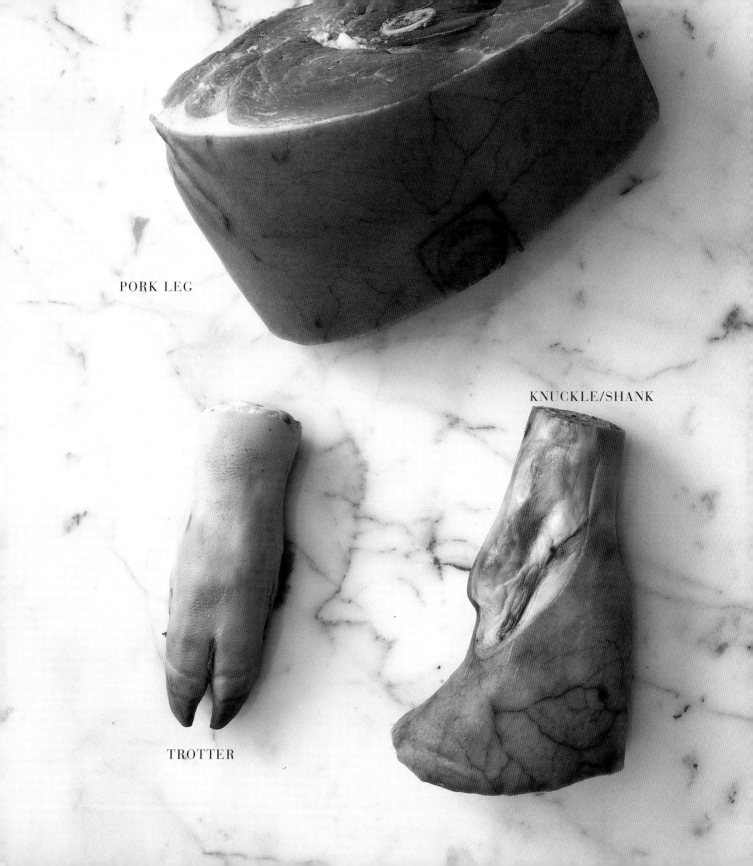

PORK LEG

KNUCKLE/SHANK

TROTTER

CUTS OF CHICKEN

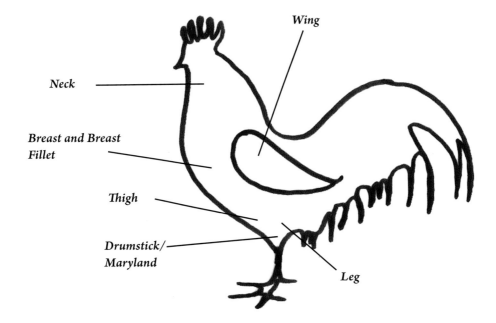

Wing

Neck

Breast and Breast
Fillet

Thigh

Drumstick/
Maryland

Leg

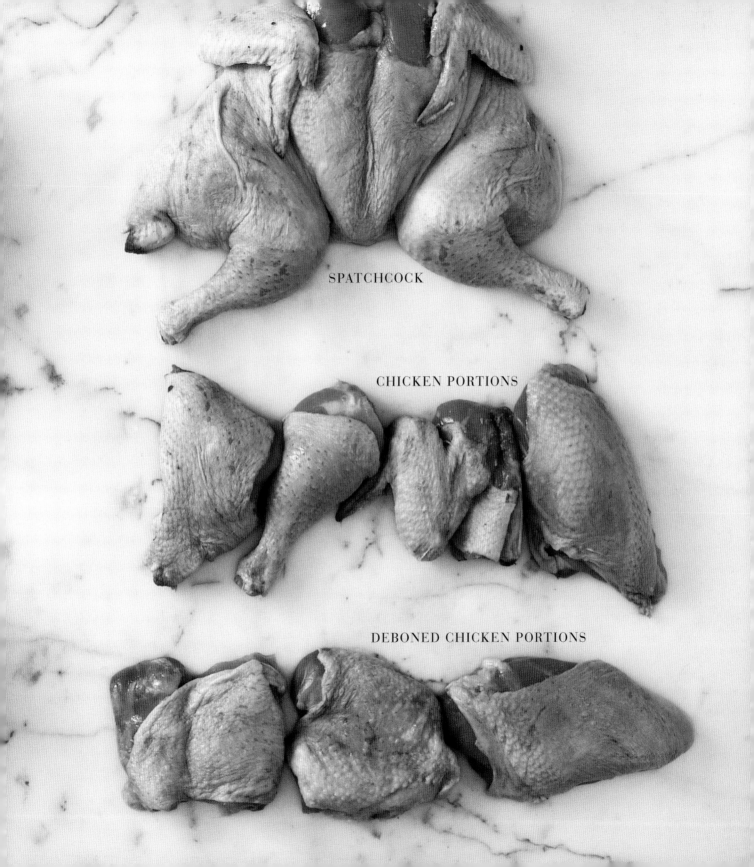

SPATCHCOCK

CHICKEN PORTIONS

DEBONED CHICKEN PORTIONS

STORING MEAT

Meat is sold refrigerated and needs to be kept chilled until it is cooked or brought to room temperature prior to cooking. All meat has a definite lifespan, after which time it will start to smell unpleasant and become unusable. Buying the freshest possible meat and refrigerating it quickly will ensure a longer lifespan. If you're in any doubt about the freshness of meat that's been in the refrigerator for a while, discard it rather than risk eating it. A slightly unpleasant odour and greying of colour are sure signs that the meat is past its best.

Storing meat correctly is important and cannot be underestimated. There are a few essential guidelines to follow when handling meat. Always wash your hands thoroughly with soap and water after touching meat to avoid transferring bacteria between produce and surfaces. Bacteria thrives naturally on raw meat, and even on cooked produce that has come into contact with raw meat. Cooking raw food kills the bacteria.

All meat needs to breathe. If you are not cooking it straight away, unwrap the meat and transfer it to a plate or tray. Ensure that the receptacle is large enough to hold all of the meat and that no blood will run off the plate onto produce stored on shelves below. Place in the refrigerator and cover loosely with greaseproof paper so air can still circulate. Ensure that no other foodstuffs stored in the refrigerator come into contact with the raw meat. Make sure that the refrigerator is set at 5°C (41°F) or lower. If you are storing cooked leftovers from roast joints, for example, ensure that they cool to room temperature before chilling them. With the exception of minced meat, offal and poultry, most meats can be stored successfully in the fridge for a few days. Beef and lamb will keep for longer than pork.

Freeze meat on the day that you purchase it and wrap it well so that no cross contamination can occur. Label with cut of meat, weight and date. (It's easy to remember what you're freezing on the day of freezing, but not so easy to distinguish it a couple of months later, particularly in its frozen state) Defrost frozen meat in the refrigerator in a container that will contain any juices that may run.

Chicken doesn't keep as well as red meats and is best used within two days of shopping. If storing for longer, make use of the freezer, returning it to the fridge the day before cooking.

EQUIPMENT

There are just a few items of equipment that are used repeatedly by the meat cook and could be described as essentials. Generally the better the quality the more robust the equipment will be and the longer it'll last.

A couple of decent knives will make chopping, slicing and general preparation enjoyable rather than frustrating. Although expensive they will last many years provided they're looked after and not put in the dishwasher to thrown in a drawer with other kitchen gadgets. Likewise a sturdy wooden chopping board that doesn't slide around on the work surface will make preparation easier and safer. If your board is a little lightweight or the surface is uneven place a teatowel underneath to keep everything stable.

Pans are another great asset that'll make frying, roasting and baking so much more pleasurable. Good quality frying pans will brown meat and vegetables without sticking or burning. You might also want to buy a ridged grill pan for cooking steaks and other pieces of meat that produce appealing and professional looking grill lines. A large heavyweight roasting tin, one that's sufficiently sturdy to be used on the hob for gravy making, will come in useful for both roasts and pot roasts. For grinding spices a pestle and mortar is the easiest choice though you can get away with using a small bowl and the end of a wooden rolling pin for lightly crushing. Finally, a food processor is so useful for making sauces and pastes and is great for mincing meat if you don't have an electrical mincer attachment on an electrical appliance, or the type of mincer that can be screwed onto the kitchen surface.

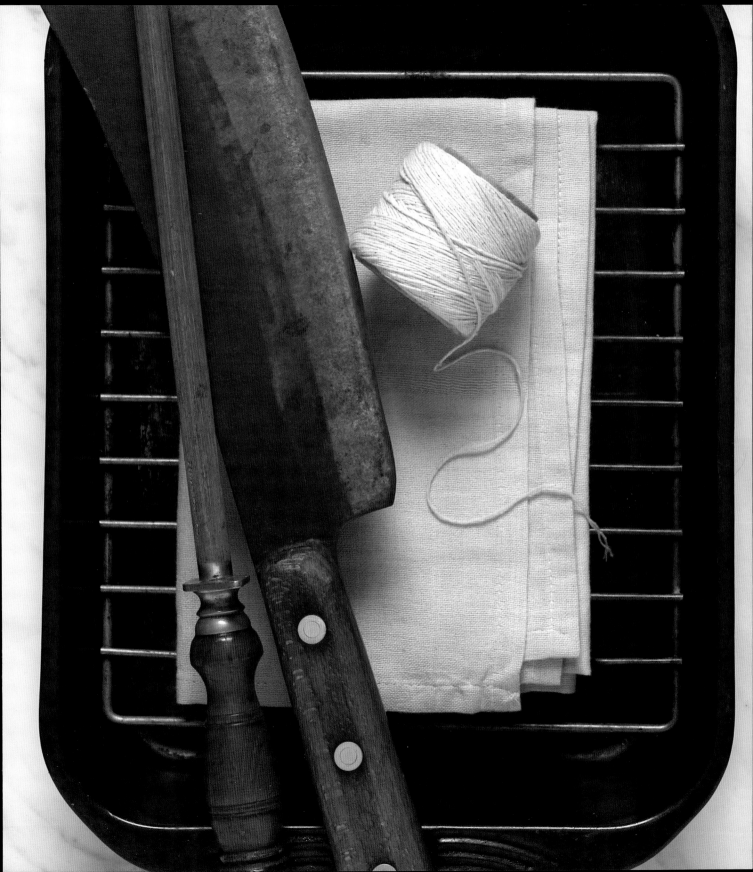

PREPARATION TECHNIQUES

Meat can be bought in various stages of 'readiness' for cooking. You might buy a large joint of beef, lamb or pork that needs a little preparation before you roast it, or a beautifully French-trimmed rack of lamb that only requires a sprinkling of seasoning before you pop it in the oven. What you buy depends largely on where you've shopped, what you're cooking and how much of the preparation you want to do yourself. For some cooks part of the pleasure is in the trimming and chopping of a particular cut, while others want to get straight down to cooking. To really feel that you've mastered the skills of meat cooking it's good to know how to tackle all the preparation techniques even if you won't be using them all the time.

Trimming excess fat

Avoid buying cuts of meat that have been trimmed of all fat. It's the fat in meat that provides its delicious flavour and succulence, particularly in slow-cooked dishes where it renders down and tenderizes as it cooks. Having said that, you don't want to choose a cut of meat in which a large proportion is fat rather than flesh since that does not represent good value for money.

The fat on most joints is under the skin. When positioning the meat in a roasting tin (pan), make sure the fat side is uppermost so that it can naturally baste the meat during cooking. Many lean meats also contain thin threads of fat running through them known as 'marbling', which is a sure sign of well-produced meat. Some cuts, such as topside and top rump, contain very little fat and are more prone to dryness. To flavour these meats and prevent them from drying out during cooking, butchers wrap them in a layer of fat, in a process known as 'barding'.

There are just a few occasions when you might want to remove some of the surface fat, for instance when roasting a fillet of beef. The strip of fat that runs through the joint can be cut away with a large, sharp knife. If the fillet is then being roasted in one piece, tie it at intervals with string to hold any loose pieces of meat in place. You might also want to cut away any loose areas of fat when dicing a shoulder of lamb, or on steaks or chops for barbecuing, as dripping fat can cause flare-ups while the meat cooks. It's also best to trim the excess fat off steak before stir-frying.

Cutting meat into chunks

Meat can be bought ready-diced for using in stews, casseroles and pies, but by doing it yourself you can be sure that you are using a decent cut of meat and can cut it to the size you want. First cut the meat away from the bone (keep the bone for stock, see page 88–89) and discard any ragged pieces of fat. Cut the meat into chunks. These don't have to be regular but 2–3 cm (¾–1¼ in) is fine for most dishes.

Making homemade mince

Bought mince is certainly convenient but by making your own you will know precisely the quality of the meat that's gone into the mince and you can choose how coarse or fine you want it to be. Meat mincers are relatively inexpensive and work well but a food processor is much easier to use and chops meat cleanly to the texture you want (take care not to over-blend or it'll be reduced to a smooth paste). The cut of meat you choose depends on what you're making. For burgers it's best to use a good-quality, lean steak mince while cheaper cuts with a little fat can be used for slow-cooked dishes. Your butcher can advise you on this.

First cut the meat into small dice by hand, including a little of the fat. Process in small batches as this will produce a more consistent texture than blending all in one go. Transfer the batches to a bowl while you mince the remainder.

You can easily make your own sausagemeat by taking your minced pork one stage further to a slightly more paste-like consistency – this is great for stuffings and pâtés.

Preparing escalopes

Escalopes are frequently made using boneless lean veal cut from the rump or topside, but the same techniques can be applied to chicken breasts, boneless leg or loin, or pork or lamb, and any beef steaks. Escalopes are made by beating slices of meat with a rolling pin to flatten into thin pieces for quick, even cooking. The beating action also breaks down the muscles to tenderize the meat. Because escalopes are fried, barbecued or grilled (broiled), you need to use more expensive cuts than you would normally buy for quick cooking.

If you've bought the meat in one piece, first cut it across the grain of the meat into slices about 1.5cm (⅝ in) thick. If using chicken breasts, first slice each horizontally in half. Allow 150–200 g (5½–7 oz) per portion. A large piece of sirloin or rump steak might simply need cutting in half to create the right-sized portions.

Place the pieces of meat on a plastic wrap-lined board, leaving at least 5 cm (2 in) between each piece. Cover with a second layer of plastic wrap. Use a rolling pin or a meat mallet to hammer the pieces to about 5 mm (¼ in) thickness.

Marinating

The purpose of a marinade is to flavour and tenderize meat by steeping it in aromatic ingredients that penetrate its surface. However, strongly flavoured or acidic marinades cannot effectively reach the centre of a large piece of meat but their delicious flavours can work their magic on the outer areas and become further enhanced during cooking. Meat can be marinated briefly (in the time it takes you to prepare other aspects of the meal) or for several hours, depending on the marinade itself and the size of the meat. A large joint might be left overnight or for a couple of days. If marinating for more than half an hour, chill the meat in its marinade, loosely covered with plastic wrap. Don't add salt to a marinade as it draws out the moisture from the meat.

Wet marinades include spicy yogurt-based ones, wine, garlic, onion, herb-flavoured vinegar; and fruit juices including pineapple, kiwi and citrus juices are effective tenderizers. If the meat is not totally immersed in the marinade you'll need to turn it occasionally so that all surfaces are flavoured. Meats that are wet-marinated are drained and patted dry on kitchen paper before cooking. Meat portions such as lamb shanks, chicken breasts or chunky pork chops can be scored through their surfaces so the marinade can reach further into the meat.

Dry marinades include aromatic herb and garlic pastes and spice blends that are rubbed into the surface of the meat and are really good for meats that are barbecued, grilled (broiled), fried or roasted. These, too, can be left for just 10–20 minutes, several hours or overnight.

Marinating tips

• Don't add salt to a wet or dry marinade as it draws out moisture from the meat. The exception to this is salted meats in which the aim is to remove moisture and change the texture of the flesh.

• For thick pieces of meat that are going to be fried, grilled (broiled) or barbecued, make cuts into the surface so that the marinade can be rubbed or absorbed into the meat to add flavour (this also speeds up cooking times).

Simple marinades

These easy marinades are great if you want to keep the meal simple, but give the meat a slightly punchier flavour. Leave in the marinade for 10–15 minutes, while you sort out the accompaniments. Each makes enough for 4 servings.

HERB, GARLIC AND LEMON MARINADE

Mix together 1 crushed garlic clove, 2 finely chopped shallots, 2 tablespoons finely chopped oregano, 2 teaspoons finely chopped rosemary or thyme, the finely grated zest of 1 lemon, 30 ml (2 tablespoons) olive oil and plenty of freshly ground black pepper. Rub over all sides of the meat.

CHICKEN TIKKA MARINADE

Mix together 2 tablespoons natural (plain) yogurt, 1 tablespoon tikka spice, 2 cm (¾ in) piece fresh root ginger, chopped, and 2 crushed garlic cloves. Turn the chicken portions in the paste.

THAI CURRY MARINADE

Mix 60 ml (4 tablespoons) coconut cream or milk with 1½ tablespoons Thai red or green curry paste and 15 ml (1 tablespoon) lime juice. Turn meat portions in the paste.

CAJUN SPICE RUB

Crush 2 teaspoons fennel seeds and mix with 1 teaspoon smoked paprika, 1 crushed garlic clove, ½ teaspoon dried oregano and a good pinch of cayenne pepper. Rub over the meat portions.

Stuffing and rolling a joint of meat

The idea of stuffing and rolling a joint of meat might be a little daunting, but the technique is simple and it means you're guaranteed a well-flavoured piece of meat even before you've started cooking. Various joints can be stuffed and rolled for roasting or pot roasting, and the stuffing provides a flavour contrast that also infuses into the meat as it cooks. Joints like lean belly, shoulder of pork or loin of lamb are ideal (if the butcher has boned the joint for you don't forget to take the bones home for stock).

Because there's little space within a joint to accommodate stuffing, it's good to use intense flavours such as garlic and herbs, capers, olives, anchovies, Indian and Asian spices, dried fruits, olives or hot spicy sausage. If the stuffing has been cooked first, leave it to cool completely before stuffing and rolling, after which time you can chill the prepared joint until ready to cook.

Arrange the joint of meat on the work surface, untying any string if the joint used has already been rolled. Make sure the outside surface of the meat is face down and have string and scissors ready for tying. Spoon the stuffing down the centre of the meat. Bring the edges of the meat up over the stuffing so that you're able to create a joint that's cylindrical in shape. Slide the string under the centre of the joint, wrap it around the meat and tie in a knot. Tie more pieces of string around the joint, leaving about 4 cm (1½ in) between each tie.

Stuffing a chicken or other bird

The cavity inside a chicken, turkey or other large bird should not be packed with stuffing as the bird would be overcooked before the stuffing had sufficient time in the oven to cook through safely. Instead, pack some stuffing into the neck cavity and pull the flap of skin around the stuffing, tucking it under the bird to hold the stuffing in place. The remaining stuffing can be rolled into balls or packed into a loaf tin (pan) and cooked separately.

If you want to add extra flavour to a roast chicken, turkey or smaller bird, push garlic cloves, shallots, onion halves, lemon quarters and sprigs of herbs into the body cavity. You can also push a well-flavoured stuffing directly under the skin, which both flavours and moistens the flesh (see page 71).

How to joint a chicken

There are several advantages to jointing a chicken before cooking. Firstly, you can make a whole substantially sized bird go a little further by jointing into ten pieces, which will serve up to five people. Secondly, you cannot readily buy a jointed chicken from a supermarket (though a good butcher will joint one for you). Thirdly, you can use the carcass to make stock or freeze the carcass to make a larger batch of stock once you've collected enough bones. This method can also be used to joint a small turkey, guinea fowl or pheasant.

1 Using a sharp knife, cut vertically down through the skin and flesh between the leg and breast on one side of the bird. Pull the leg away from the body until the ball and socket joint at the carcass end of the thigh is exposed. Bend the leg back so the joint snaps apart, then use the tip of the knife to release the meat around the joint. Before releasing the leg completely, try to locate the 'oyster'. This is a small, fleshly (and very tasty) oval-shaped piece of meat that's attached to the thigh meat but nestles in the backbone. Use the tip of the knife to scoop out this piece of meat. Repeat on the other side.

2 To make the wing portions meatier and worthy of portioning, a small piece of breast meat can be removed with them. Hold the wing and make a diagonal cut down through the back of the breast. Feel around for the wing joint with your knife until you find the socket. Cut through this and remove completely. Repeat on the other side.

3 Cut vertically down one side of the breastbone, keeping the knife against the rib cage to avoid wasting any meat. Pull the breast meat back with one hand as you ease the flesh away from the ribs with a knife until you can release the whole breast in one piece. Repeat on the other side.

4 Place a leg joint, skin side down on the board. Bend the leg to give you an idea of where the joint is located (there's usually a thin piece of white fat over the joint where you need to aim the knife). Cut down through this to divide the leg into two pieces. Sometimes this happens very easily, other times you might need to wiggle the knife slightly each way until you can feel it cutting easily through the joint. Repeat with the other leg.

5 Cut each breast portion across into two pieces.

6 If a recipe calls for skinned chicken pieces, pull away and discard all the skin and any lumpy pieces of fat after jointing. The drumstick is the trickiest portion to skin. The easiest way to do this is to pull the skin back over the thin end and firmly tug it away from the meat. If your hand is slipping, use kitchen paper to get a firm grip on the skin.

Roasting

R oasting is one of the least labour-intensive ways to cook meat. If you feel that roasting requires advanced skills that you cannot achieve, think again. All the perfect roast requires is a beautiful piece of meat and a few basic pointers in the right direction.

The perfect roast is crisp and golden on the outside, juicy and succulent within, and, for the dedicated meat connoisseur, preferably still a little pink. Meat can be roasted on the bone, which speeds up cooking time slightly as the bone conducts heat; it also impregnates the meat with extra flavour. If you're apprehensive about carving a joint at the table, buy a boned one to make slicing easy. Most boned joints are also rolled and tied with string to make a neat shape, which makes carving easier still. If possible, buy a larger joint than you need for the number of diners; not only will this provide plenty of delicious leftovers for the next day, but a large roast produces even more precious juices for making delicious gravy.

Roasting tips

- Have the oven really hot before you start so that when you put the joint in, the meat contracts quickly, forcing juices to bubble up to the surface. These crisp and caramelize the surface, producing a tasty, flavour-packed crust.

- Ideally, meat should be cooked from room temperature so the heat penetrates quickly through to the centre. If this isn't convenient, or you've forgotten to remove the meat from the refrigerator, it can still be roasted successfully although you might need to lengthen the cooking time slightly.

- Have any sauces and dressings ready before starting, and plan the cooking times for accompaniments. Don't worry about gravy yet as this is made while the meat is resting (see page 45).

- A successful roast needn't be served with lavish accompaniments or additional flavourings. A few basic additions, such as garlic and rosemary for lamb or mustard for beef, enhance the meat's flavour but are not essential. Another effective technique is to slice a couple of onions and mix with several sprigs of herbs such as rosemary, thyme, parsley, sage or fennel and place under the joint before roasting. This helps flavour both meat and juices for gravy.

- Always place the meat in the roasting tin (pan) with fat side uppermost so that the fat bastes the meat as it cooks.

- If you're roasting a boned joint of meat and you've asked the butcher for the bones as well, use these as a base for the meat. Put them in the tin, maybe with a scattering of sliced onion, garlic cloves and herb sprigs, then rest the meat on top. The bones will flavour the meat and juices. After roasting you'll have ready-browned bones for making stock (see page 188–189).

- If you're roasting a stuffed joint, weigh the meat after stuffing to calculate the cooking time.
- You might want to prepare your joint for roasting a little in advance, particularly if you're entertaining. Tie up, stuff, or add other flavours to the joint. Don't season with salt until just before cooking as it draws out moisture from the meat.

Crisping the skin

The skin of a good-quality roasting pork joint crisps easily and deliciously to make perfect crackling (see page 63). For roast lamb and beef, rub the surface of the joint with a little seasoned flour just before you pop it in the oven, which gives a good crust and flavour. For roast beef, use a half-and-half mix of flour and dry mustard.

Joints can also be basted during cooking by spooning the fat that accumulates in the roasting tin (pan) over the surface of the meat. The purpose of basting is to keep the meat moist and juicy as it roasts, counteracting the effects of the dry heat. However, if you are roasting a decent joint of meat with a good covering of fat, the meat bastes naturally as it cooks. The skin of roast chicken can be basted several times during cooking as there's little natural fat under the skin.

When to use a roasting rack

Roasting racks, often included when you buy a roasting tin, are generally only needed for cooking very fatty cuts of meat. This usually applies only to roast duck, goose or slow-roasted joints such as a slow-roasted belly of lamb; otherwise, the meat sits directly in the pan. This helps produce lovely caramelly gravy juices and it's easy to drain off the excess fat after roasting (see page 45).

How to test if meat is cooked

Having bought and roasted a quality piece of meat, the last thing you want to do is overcook it – the meat will start to dry out and all the delicious juiciness will be lost. Calculate the roasting time and check the joint slightly before this time is up. Do this by pushing a skewer into the thickest area of the meat. Remove the skewer and press it against the meat. If the juices that run out are still red, the meat is rare, if pink the meat is medium-cooked and if clear then the meat is cooked through. For chicken and turkey, which must be cooked through, pierce the thickest part of the thigh with a skewer. Remove the skewer and press it against the meat so the juices run out. If the juices are clear then the bird is cooked but if at all pink, return the bird to the oven for a while longer. Use the same test for small game birds, or, for a quicker method, pull away one of the legs, which should come away easily.

A more accurate way of gauging how well the meat is cooked is to use a meat thermometer that reads the internal temperature of the meat. These are inexpensive and provide you with an accurate way of checking that the meat is cooked just as you want it. Remove the joint or bird from the oven and push the thermometer into the thickest area of the joint, but away from any bone. Leave for about 15 seconds before reading the temperature. Perfectly cooked joints should read as follows:

Rare beef or lamb 50°C (120°F)
Medium beef or lamb 60°C (140°F)
Well done beef or lamb 75°C (165°F)
Veal 70°C (158°F)
Pork 75°C (165°F)
Chicken and turkey 82°C (180°F)

Roasting times

In order to calculate the roasting times, first weigh the uncooked joint after adding any stuffing you are using. For accurate times see the chart below. Roast in a preheated oven at 220°C/425°F/Gas mark 7 for 30 minutes, then reduce the oven temperature to 180°C/350°F/Gas mark 4 and roast for the times indicated below. These times are for meat cooked from room temperatures so you'll need to add a little extra time if roasting chilled meats. To test if meat is cooked, see above.

Beef or lamb, rare	10–12 minutes per 500 g (1 lb 2 oz)
Beef or lamb, medium	15–18 minutes per 500 g (1 lb 2 oz)
Beef or lamb, well done	20–25 minutes per 500 g (1 lb 2 oz)
Veal	15–18 minutes per 500 g (1 lb 2 oz)
Pork	25–30 minutes per 500 g (1 lb 2 oz)
Venison, medium	15–18 minutes per 500 g (1 lb 2 oz)
Chicken, guinea fowl, or pheasant	20 minutes per 500 g (1 lb 2 oz)
Turkey	20 minutes per 500 g (1 lb 2 oz) decreasing to 15 minutes per 500 g (1 lb 2 oz) for turkeys over 4.5 kg (10 lb)
Duck	25 minutes per 500 g (1 lb 2 oz)

Resting meat

Loosely covering the joint or bird with foil and allowing it to 'rest' is essential for serving meat at its most tender and succulent and also makes it easier to carve. During cooking the dry, intense heat makes the meat contract, pushing the juices to the surface. Once the meat is removed from the oven, the reverse happens and the juices 'relax' back into the meat as it rests. Transfer the meat to a board or surface that you're going to carve it on, cover with foil and leave in a warm place. Rest a large roast for 30–40 minutes; slightly less time for a smaller one. This allows a bit of time to cook vegetables, to turn up the oven if necessary to finish the roast potatoes and, of course, to make gravy.

How to make perfect gravy

Gravy-making starts with a process called 'deglazing', which simply means scraping the roasting pan over heat on the stove top (once the joint has been removed) with the addition of some liquid. In the bottom of the pan you'll have an intensely flavoured mixture of caramelized juices, meat fat and any other flavours you've added to the roasting tin (pan) such as bits of garlic, onion and herbs. These will all contribute to your perfect gravy.

Before you begin the deglazing process, check to see if there's an excessive amount of fat left in the pan once the joint is removed. Pork, lamb and duck produce the most. Tilt the pan so the fat accumulates in one corner, and if there is more than a couple of tablespoons skim it off with a spoon, taking care not to remove any of the meaty juices that collect under the fat (keep the fat from beef or duck for roasting potatoes another time, or for cooking Yorkshire puddings).

Pour a dash of wine, stock (or a mixture of both) into the juices left in the pan and heat over the stove top, stirring and scraping the pan residues with a wooden spoon. Continue to stir as the liquid starts to bubble up and thicken, adding more liquid until you have your required amount for gravy. Taste to check the seasoning and add more if necessary. If the gravy tastes a little thin you can continue to let it bubble away to reduce and intensify. Strain the gravy through a sieve into a gravy boat to serve.

POT ROASTING

Pot roasting is a method of cooking joints of meat with vegetables, herbs and spices and a small amount of liquid. Low cooking temperatures and moist heat enable you to use cheaper or tougher cuts of meat that would not be sufficiently tender if fast roasted. You can use additional ingredients, particularly aromatics such as garlic, ginger, spices and herbs that complement your chosen meat. Combined with a well-flavoured stock, wine, beer or cider, these flavours have plenty of time to develop and mingle. Like slow roasting, pot roasting allows you to leave dinner unattended for several hours with the reassurance that you'll return to a delicious, tender roast that won't have overcooked. Even better, the cooking liquid will have absorbed all the meaty flavours to provide an integral gravy. Pot roasting does not produce roasts that are pink in the middle though you can still make a decent crackling (see page 63).

A large sturdy casserole dish is ideal for pot roasting but if you don't have one use a deep-sided roasting tin (pan) instead, covered with foil if the recipe requires. Most meats are seared in hot oil first to caramelize the surface and add colour and flavour. Do this in a frying pan or in the casserole dish (or roasting tin) if it is sturdy enough.

Pot roasting tips

- Invest in a good-quality flameproof casserole dish with a lid so you can do the frying and cooking all in one pot.
- Use good-quality stock, preferably homemade. If using wine, it needn't be the best but should be one you'd drink.
- Long, slow cooking times ensure that the meat is cooked through so timings needn't be as accurate as for fast roasting.
- If the pot roast is cooked but you're not quite ready to eat, turn the oven down to its lowest setting, or even off as it'll keep hot for up to an hour. This also gives you time to finish any accompaniments.
- Always serve an accompaniment that'll mop up all the delicious juices. Choose a carbohydrate that complements the dish such as mashed potatoes, rice, noodles, polenta or even chunks of bread.

SLOW ROASTING

Slow roasting produces some of the most delicious and mouthwatering meat dishes. The meat cooks very gently, sometimes for six or seven hours, until it is so soft that it simply falls apart in juicy morsels. Slow-roasted joints cannot be cooked rare, and fatty meats such as lamb, pork and duck give the best results. Pricier cuts including leg and loin can be slow-roasted but those cuts which have fat dispersed within the meat, like belly and shoulder, make the best, most succulent slow roasts of all.

Slow-roasted joints are put in a hot oven for about 30 minutes then turned down to a low temperature and simply left to cook. Because you don't need to tend the meat throughout cooking, slow roasts make the perfect solution if you're going to be out and about, and want to return to a delicious roast that's ready and waiting for you. They are also great if you're entertaining and don't feel confident about having your guests sitting down and ready to eat at a planned time. Long, gentle cooking means that the meat won't overcook, even if you eat an hour or so later than you intended.

The natural flavours that develop in a slow roast mean that you need barely any other additional ingredients, though a bed of herbs, garlic or spice rub can still enhance the finished roast. The meat is cooked dry as in a traditional roast (if liquid is added it then becomes a pot roast, see page 46). Accompaniments can be the same as for a traditional roast. If you want to serve roast potatoes, cook them gently over the meat for an hour or so and then turn up the heat once the meat has been removed. It is not necessary to rest the meat as you would for a hot, fast roast, though you can cover the meat and leave it to stand while the gravy and accompaniments are being finished.

pot-roasted beef with coconut and spices

Topside of beef is a good choice for pot roasting. Here it is cooked slowly and gently to tenderize and absorb the well-flavoured Asian spices. Serve with fine or ribbon noodles..

Serves 6

1 teaspoon each of ground cumin, coriander
   and paprika

½ teaspoon salt

1.5 kg (3 lb 5 oz) beef topside

30 ml (2 tablespoons) vegetable oil

4 garlic cloves, chopped

1 medium-hot green chilli, deseeded
   and thinly sliced

50 g (2 oz) fresh root ginger, peeled and chopped

150 ml (5 fl oz) beef or chicken stock

2 lemongrass stalks, ends removed and discarded,
   and stalks finely chopped

30 ml (2 tablespoons) Thai fish sauce (nam pla)

3 tablespoons caster (superfine) sugar

30 ml (2 tablespoons) lime juice

40 g (1½ oz) fresh coriander (cilantro)

1 bunch spring onions (scallions)

400 g (14 oz) tin coconut milk

Preheat the oven to 150°C/300°F/Gas mark 2. Mix together the ground cumin, coriander, paprika and salt, and rub all over the surfaces of the beef. Heat the oil in a large flameproof casserole. Once hot, add the beef and sear quickly on all sides, including the ends, turning the beef as each area is browned.

Position the beef so the fat side is uppermost. Scatter the garlic, chilli and ginger around the beef and cook for another minute. Pour in the stock and bring to the boil. Cover with a lid or foil and transfer to the oven. Cook for 2½ hours.

Cut off the tip at the thick end of the lemongrass and at the thin end where it starts to look straw like. Slice the lemongrass as thinly as possible. Put in a blender or food processor with the fish sauce, sugar, lime juice, fresh coriander and spring onions. Blend until the ingredients are finely chopped. Add the coconut milk and blend until the mixture has a soupy consistency and is specked with green.

Lift the beef from the dish. If a thick layer of fat has accumulated on top of the meat juices, spoon it off by tilting the dish so the liquid gathers on one side. Spoon out the fat making sure you retain all the meaty juices underneath. Return the meat to the dish.

Pour the coconut mixture over the beef and return to the oven for another 15 minutes. Leave to stand for 10 minutes then snip off the string and serve in thin slices with the sauce spooned over.

roast beef with yorkshire pudding

This weight of beef will provide six generous portions but you can easily use a smaller or larger joint to suit your requirements. Roast a larger joint if you want leftovers. It's best to keep accompaniments simple particularly if you're inexperienced with roasting. Roast potatoes are a 'must have', see recipe on page 198. Serve one or two seasonal green vegetables too, which you can prepare in advance so that they're ready to cook while the meat is resting.

Serves 6

2.5 kg (5½ lb) rib or sirloin of beef on the bone
    (or boned and rolled), at room temperature
2 teaspoons dry mustard
2 teaspoons plain (all-purpose) flour
200 ml (7 fl oz) red wine
200 ml (7 fl oz) beef stock
salt and freshly ground black pepper

FOR THE YORKSHIRE PUDDINGS
125 g (4½ oz) plain (all-purpose) flour
2 medium eggs
300 ml (10 fl oz) milk
a little lard or beef dripping

Preheat the oven to 220°C/425°F/Gas mark 7. Weigh the meat and calculate the cooking time (see page 44). Place in the roasting tin (pan) with the fat side uppermost. Mix together the mustard, flour and salt and pepper and rub it all over the fat.

Roast for 30 minutes, then reduce the oven temperature to 180°C/350°F/Gas mark 4 and roast for the calculated cooking time.

Meanwhile make the batter for the Yorkshire puddings: sift the flour into a bowl and make a well in the centre. Break the eggs into the well and add a little of the milk. Whisk the eggs and milk to combine, gradually working in the flour until the mixture starts to thicken. Pour in the remaining milk as you whisk and continue until the batter is smooth. Alternatively, you can mix all the ingredients in a food processor for a couple of minutes until smooth. Pour into a measuring jug (pitcher) for easy pouring.

Test that the meat is roasted to your taste (see page 44), and transfer to a carving platter or board. Cover with foil and leave to rest in a warm place for 30 minutes.

Raise the oven temperature to 220°C/425°F/Gas mark 7. Dot a little lard, dripping, or drained fat from the roasting tin (pan) into a 12-section Yorkshire pudding tin. Put in the oven and heat until the fat is melted and very hot (it's vital that the fat is very hot before adding the batter or the puddings won't rise). Pour the batter into the cups. If the fat doesn't sizzle when you add the batter it is not hot enough so return the tin to the oven for a couple more minutes.

Cook the puddings in the oven for 20–25 minutes until well risen, crisp and golden.

While the puddings are cooking, make the gravy. If you haven't used the fat from the roasting tin for the Yorkshire puddings, drain off any excess (see page 45). Pour a little wine into the roasting tin and stir over the stove top, scraping up the pan sediment and all the crispy bits until the juices start to bubble. Pour in the remaining wine and stock and cook, stirring frequently for about 10 minutes until slightly reduced and thickened. Season to taste with salt and pepper and strain through a sieve into a gravy boat.

roast lamb with garlic and rosemary

Garlic and rosemary are classic flavourings for a joint of lamb and can be pushed into slits in the surface of the fat so that the flavours of the herbs penetrate the meat as it cooks. A large leg of lamb is a good choice for a crowd and can be served pink in the middle. A rack of lamb on the bone, or boned and rolled, makes a good choice for a smaller gathering, though you can, of course, cook two or three racks in the same tin. Shoulder of lamb is best slow-roasted so the layers of fat can melt into the meat as it cooks. Serve with roast potatoes or minted new potatoes, depending on the time of year, and seasonal vegetables.

Serves 6–8

1 large leg of lamb, about 2.5 kg (5½ lb), bone in

plenty of sprigs of rosemary

5 garlic cloves, crushed

a little olive oil

1 teaspoon plain (all-purpose) flour

300 ml (10 fl oz pint) dry white wine

45 ml (3 tablespoons) redcurrant jelly (jam)

salt and freshly ground black pepper

Preheat the oven to 220°C/425°F/Gas mark 7. Weigh the meat and calculate the cooking time (see page 44). Using the tip of a small sharp knife, make numerous deep slits over the plump, fattier side of the leg.

Pull the leaves from some of the rosemary sprigs and chop them until you have a generous tablespoonful. Mix on the board with the crushed garlic and salt and pepper. Push the mixture into the slits and spread any excess over the surface of the lamb. Place the lamb in a roasting tin (pan) with any remaining rosemary sprigs and bits of garlic pushed underneath the joint.

Drizzle the surface with a little olive oil and season generously with salt and pepper. Roast for 20 minutes then reduce the temperature to 180°C/350°F/Gas mark 4 and continue roasting for the calculated cooking time.

Test that the meat is roasted to your taste (see page 44), and transfer to a carving platter or board. Cover with foil and leave to rest in a warm place for 20–30 minutes.

To make the gravy, drain off the excess fat from the roasting tin. Place the tin over a gentle heat and sprinkle in the flour. Stir well, scraping up the pan juices and meat residue. Once the flour has started to colour, gradually pour in the wine, stirring as the gravy starts to bubble up. Add the redcurrant jelly and continue to stir until the gravy is slightly thickened and the redcurrant jelly has melted. Season to taste with salt and pepper. Strain through a sieve into a gravy boat and serve with the lamb.

Tip

A roasted rack of lamb makes a good choice for a smaller group. A large French-trimmed rack of 7 ribs will serve 2–3, or you could roast 2 racks for 5–6 servings. Drizzle the fat sides with olive oil and sprinkle with salt, pepper and a little finely chopped thyme. Roast in a preheated oven at 200°C/400°F/Gas mark 6 for 25 minutes before testing to see whether it's cooked to your taste (see page 44). Cook a little longer if necessary, then rest the meat and make gravy as above.

marinated rack of lamb

Racks of lamb cook comparatively quickly so you'll need to be organized with accompanying vegetables, such as new potatoes and roasted tomatoes, before you put the lamb in the oven. This makes a lovely summer roast. Ask the butcher to French-trim the lamb for you.

Serves 4

several sprigs of thyme, leaves removed

10 g (¼ oz) each of parsley, fresh coriander (cilantro) and mint, roughly torn

1 garlic clove, roughly chopped

1 teaspoon cumin seeds

1 medium-hot red chilli, deseeded and roughly chopped

60 ml (4 tablespoons) mild olive oil

15 ml (1 tablespoon) sherry or white wine vinegar

15 ml (1 tablespoon) clear honey

salt

2 small 'French-trimmed' racks of lamb (each about 6–7 ribs), each cut into even portions of 2 or 3 ribs.

To make the marinade, put the thyme leaves in a food processor with the parsley, coriander, mint, garlic, cumin seeds, chilli, olive oil, vinegar and honey. Blend briefly to make a paste.

Put the lamb ribs in a non-metallic container. Tip the mixture out onto the lamb and spread over all the meat so that it is evenly covered. Cover loosely with plastic wrap and chill for several hours.

Preheat the oven to 220°C/425°F/Gas mark 7. Lift the meat from the marinade, scraping off the excess. Heat a large frying pan without any oil until very hot. Add a couple of pieces of the lamb and brown briefly, turning until the pieces are coloured on all sides. Drain to a roasting tin (pan) arranging the lamb so the fat sides are uppermost, then brown the remainder and add to the tin.

Roast the lamb for 25 minutes, then test the pieces to ensure that they are cooked to your taste (see page 44). Lamb racks vary in size and therefore cooking times will also vary. As a guide, allow 20 minutes for rare, 25 minutes for medium and 30 minutes for well done. Leave to rest in a warm place for 15 minutes before serving.

indian-style
shoulder of lamb

This is a really delicious pot roast. The lamb is marinated in a spicy yogurt paste and then cooked on a bed of onions until it is meltingly tender. The flavour is spicy but not too hot. Serve with basmati rice.

Serves 6

1 large shoulder of lamb, boned and rolled

12 cardamom pods, crushed, shells removed

1 teaspoon coarse ground black pepper

2 teaspoons coriander seeds

2 teaspoons fennel seeds

½ teaspoon ground turmeric

½ teaspoon ground cinnamon

¼ teaspoon ground cloves

1 hot red chilli, deseeded and chopped

200 ml (7 fl oz) Greek (strained plain) yogurt

2 garlic cloves, crushed

3 onions, thinly sliced

1 teaspoon salt

Using a sharp knife, score the top of the lamb, parallel with the string. Make each cut about 1 cm (½ in) deep and space the cuts about 2 cm (¾ in) apart.

Put the cardamom seeds in a pestle and mortar. Add the pepper, coriander and fennel seeds and crush the spices together. Tip into a bowl. Add the ground spices, chilli, yogurt and garlic.

Put the lamb in a non-metallic container and spread the mixture all over the meat, making sure you work it into the cuts in the lamb. Cover loosely and refrigerate for 2–3 hours.

Preheat the oven to 200°C/400°F/Gas mark 6. Scatter the onions in a large casserole dish or roasting tin (pan) and put the lamb on top. Sprinkle with the salt and roast for 30 minutes.

Pour 300 ml (10 fl oz) boiling water around the lamb and reduce the oven temperature to 140°C/275°F/Gas mark 1. Cover with a lid or foil and return to the oven for 4–5 hours or until the lamb is tender (test by pulling a small piece from the joint – it should come away easily).

Transfer the lamb to a warmed serving dish, snipping off the string. Tilt the pan so the liquid gathers in one corner and drain off the fat, retaining the meaty juices and onions. Transfer to a serving bowl and serve with the lamb.

breast of lamb
with north african spices

Although slow-roasted belly pork has become very popular, recipes for the equivalent cut of lamb are seen less, even though the taste and texture is so good. When you order the joints from the butcher, ask him to roll them– you'll need to unroll them to layer in the stuffing but it'll give you an idea of how it to re-roll it.

Serves 6

15 ml (1 tablespoon) olive oil

1 small onion, chopped

3 garlic cloves, finely chopped

50 g (2 oz) pine nuts

2 teaspoons ras el hanout spice blend

3 tablespoons chopped fresh coriander (cilantro)

2 tablespoons chopped mint

25 g (1 oz) sultanas (golden raisins), chopped

salt and freshly ground black pepper

rolled breast of lamb joint, weighing about 1.75 kg
  (3 ½ lb)

2 teaspoons plain (all-purpose) flour

300 ml (10 fl oz) dry white wine

1 tablespoons clear honey

Heat the oil in a small frying pan and gently fry the onion for 3–4 minutes to soften. Add the garlic, pine nuts and ras el hanout and cook for another minute. Remove from the heat and add the coriander, mint, sultanas and a little seasoning. Leave to cool. Preheat the oven to 220°C/425°F/Gas mark 7. Cut the string of the lamb so that you're able to open the meat out without completely losing its shape. Spoon the stuffing between the layers of meat and re-tie the joint with more string.

   Place in a roasting tin (pan) and cook for 30 minutes. Reduce the oven temperature to 140°C/275°F/Gas mark 1 and cook the lamb for another 5 hours until meltingly tender. Transfer to a carving platter or board and let stand for 15 minutes before removing the string.

   To make the gravy, drain off the excess fat from the roasting tin. Place the tin over a gentle heat, add the flour and stir well, scraping up the pan sediment. Gradually blend in the wine and keep stirring until the gravy is slightly thickened and bubbling. Stir in the honey. Season to taste and strain into a gravy boat.

pancetta-wrapped roast venison

Wrapping lean venison in pancetta gives extra flavour and stops it drying out during roasting. This simple roast is lovely with mashed or roast potatoes and seasonal green vegetables.

Serves 6

2 bay leaves

6 juniper berries

½ teaspoon each of salt and pepper

1 kg (2 lb 4 oz) venison loin

175 g (6 oz) pancetta, thinly sliced

150 ml (5 fl oz) chicken or game stock

150 ml (5 fl oz) red wine

3 tablespoons blackberry jelly (jam)

Preheat the oven to 220°C/425°F/Gas mark 7. Crumble the bay leaves and grind as finely as possible using a pestle and mortar with the juniper and salt and pepper (alternatively, use a small coffee grinder).

Rub the venison all over with the seasoned mixture. Wrap a pancetta rasher around the venison, tucking the ends underneath. Wrap the remaining rashers around the venison so the joint is completely covered, apart from the ends.

Place in a roasting tin (pan) and roast for 20 minutes. Reduce the temperature to 180°C/350°F/Gas mark 4 and roast for another 30 minutes. This will give a 'slightly pink in the centre' roast. Add another 15 minutes if you prefer the venison cooked through.

Transfer the venison to a carving platter or board, cover with foil and leave to rest for 20 minutes in a warm place. Add the stock, wine and blackberry jelly to the roasting tin and cook over the stove top, stirring with a wooden spoon until hot and bubbling. Let the mixture bubble for a couple of minutes to thicken slightly. Strain into a gravy boat and serve with the thickly sliced venison.

roast pork with apple, sage and bacon stuffing

A fruity, salty stuffing is delicious with roast pork as it balances the richness of the meat. A loin or chump end works well as it makes good crackling and is not too fatty for quick roasting. Ask the butcher to bone the joint and provide you with the bones. In this recipe the bones are used as a well-flavoured 'rack' for the joint to rest on during roasting. Afterwards, use the roasted bones to make stock for another time (see page 188–189). Serve with roast potatoes and vegetables such as buttered cabbage and leeks.

Serves 6

25 g (1 oz) butter

4 rashers (strips) smoked streaky (fatty)
    bacon, diced

1 fennel bulb, chopped

2 teaspoons fennel seeds, crushed

2 garlic cloves, crushed

1 small cooking apple, peeled, cored and diced

2 tablespoons chopped sage

sea salt and freshly ground black pepper

2 kg (4 lb 8 oz) boned pork loin, spare rib
    or chump end

1 teaspoon plain (all-purpose) flour

400 ml (14 fl oz) strong cider

apple sauce to serve (see page190)

Melt the butter in a frying pan and gently fry the bacon and fennel for 10 minutes or until soft and golden. Tip into a bowl and stir in the fennel seeds, garlic, diced apple, chopped sage and a little salt and pepper. Leave to cool.

    Preheat the oven to 220°C/425°F/Gas mark 7. Arrange the pork, skin side down, on a board and spread the stuffing out over the fleshy side. Roll the pork up and secure at 4 cm (1½ in) intervals with string (see page 37). Weigh the joint to calculate the cooking time (see page 44). Rub plenty of salt into the skin.

    Place the pork bones (if you have them) in a roasting tin (pan) and put the pork on top. If not, place the pork directly in the tin.

Roast for 30 minutes then reduce the oven temperature to 180°C/350°F/Gas mark 4 and roast for the calculated time.

Test that the meat is cooked and transfer to a carving platter or board. Cover with foil and leave to rest in a warm place for 20–30 minutes. Remove the pork bones from the roasting tin and reserve for stock.

To make the gravy, drain off the excess fat from the roasting tin. Place the tin over a gentle heat and add in the flour. Stir well, scraping up the pan juices and meat residue. Once the flour has started to colour, gradually pour in the cider, stirring as the gravy starts to bubble up. Let the gravy boil for about 5 minutes until slightly reduced and thickened. Season to taste with salt and pepper. Strain through a sieve into a gravy boat and serve with the pork.

Making good crackling

You'll only get crackling from a good-quality joint of pork with a decent layer of fat under the skin. Once you've got the joint home, store it in the refrigerator so that the skin is uppermost and uncovered. Make sure the butcher has scored the skin for you. If it hasn't been scored you can do this yourself by cutting right through the skin at 1 cm (½ in) intervals with a sharp blade knife or similar DIY knife.

Just before roasting, rub the skin with plenty of sea salt, pushing the salt right into the scored skin. Put the joint in the oven and roast for 30 minutes at 220°C/425°F/Gas mark 7 to get the crackling going, before reducing the oven temperature and cooking the pork for the calculated time.

When you remove the roast from the oven, if the crackling is not as crisp as you'd hoped, slice it off the meat in one piece and return it to a hot oven for another 15–20 minutes until crisped. Crackling is easiest to serve if it is detached from the joint, so do this before serving and break it into pieces with a sharp knife, kitchen scissors, or your fingers.

smokey pulled pork with rhubarb butter

'Pulled' refers to the way the pork can simply be taken from the bone in soft succulent pieces without the need for carving. Serve hot with this tangy fruit butter. It's great for outdoor entertaining packed into bread rolls, in the same way as you'd serve hot dogs.

Serves 8

4 garlic cloves, crushed

handful of thyme leaves

salt and freshly ground black pepper

2.5 kg (5 lb 8 oz) pork shoulder

FOR THE RHUBARB BUTTER

400 g (14 oz) rhubarb

good pinch of ground cloves

75 g (2½ oz) caster (superfine) sugar

75 g (2½ oz) unsalted butter

Preheat the oven to 220°C/425°F/Gas mark 7. Pull some of the thyme leaves from the stalks until you have about 1 tablespoon. Mix the thyme with the garlic and a little salt and pepper. Use a small sharp knife to cut lots of deep slits through the pork skin and into the meat. Pack the garlic mixture into the slits.

Scatter the remaining thyme into the tin (pan) and place the meat on top, skin side uppermost. Sprinkle the skin with salt and rub it in firmly. Roast the pork for 30 minutes, then reduce the oven temperature to 140°C/275°F/Gas mark 1 and roast for another 4–5 hours.

While roasting make the rhubarb butter so it has time to chill and thicken. Trim the rhubarb and cut into 1 cm (½ in) pieces. Put in a saucepan with 15 ml (1 tablespoon) water, the cloves and sugar. Heat gently until the sugar dissolves, stirring frequently. Continue to cook gently until the rhubarb is tender and pulpy. Tip into a bowl and slice in the butter. Stir until the butter melts then leave to cool. Refrigerate until needed.

Once the pork is cooked, slice off the crackling in one piece and break it into pieces with a knife or your fingers. Pull the pork into pieces with a knife and fork and serve with the crackling and rhubarb butter.

pot-roasted pork with cider and prunes

Pork is such a versatile meat that you can use several different cuts successfully for pot-roasting including lean belly or loin. For this recipe use hand or shoulder and ask your butcher to bone and roll it for you.

Serves 6

2 teaspoons caraway seeds, crushed

2 teaspoons fennel seeds, crushed

3 garlic cloves, crushed

salt and freshly ground black pepper

2.5 kg (5 lb 8 oz) rolled hand or shoulder of pork,
    skin attached and scored

2 onions, sliced

2 celery sticks, chopped

2 teaspoons plain (all-purpose) flour

300 ml (10 fl oz) dry cider

10–12 sage leaves, torn into pieces

2 tablespoons light muscovado (brown) sugar

100 g (3½ oz) pitted prunes

Preheat the oven to 220°C/425°F/Gas mark 7. Mix the crushed caraway and fennel seeds with the garlic and a little salt and pepper and rub over the skin of the pork, pushing it right into the scored skin. Place in a roasting tin (pan), skin side uppermost. Roast for 30 minutes then remove from the oven and reduce the temperature to 140°C/275°F/Gas mark 1.

Remove the pork from the tin and set aside. Add the onions and celery to the tin and gently fry on the stove top for 5 minutes to soften. Sprinkle in the flour and stir for 1 minute. Gradually blend in the cider, stirring continuously for a couple of minutes until the liquid is smooth and thickened and no lumps of flour remain. Stir in the remaining ingredients.

Return the pork to the pan and bake, uncovered, for another 4 hours. Cut off the string holding the meat in shape and season the juices to taste before serving the pork, thickly sliced with the vegetables and cooking juices spooned over.

Preparing a chicken or turkey for roasting

Other than rinsing out and seasoning the outside of the bird, no other essential preparation is necessary. Removing the wishbone, which makes the breast meat easier to slice, is not difficult, and learning to truss the bird, which holds it in a compact shape while it is in the oven, are finishing touches rather than necessities, but it is always useful to know how to do them.

To prepare a bird for cooking, remove it from the refrigerator a couple of hours before roasting so that it has time to come to room temperature. Check for any stray feathers and pull them out using your fingers or tweezers. Rinse out the cavity under cold running water and let the water drain off before wiping out the cavity with kitchen paper. Pull out and discard any loose bits of fat from within the cavity.

To remove the wishbone: Lift the skin from around the neck cavity and run your finger along the edge of the breast meat to locate the wishbone. Scrape the meat away from the bone with a small knife then tuck the knife around the back of the thin bone so it's clearly visible. Use your fingers to lift and twist the bone free.

To truss a bird: Stuff the bird first if the recipe requires (see page 37), or simply pack a small bunch of herbs, garlic cloves and halved onion into the cavity.

Tuck the neck flap under the bird and fold the wing tips underneath the bird to keep the shape compact.

Slide a long piece of string under the bird and bring the ends up on each side between the legs and wings. Take the string back between the legs and breast meat and hook the string under the ends of the drumsticks, bringing them around to the cavity. Loop the ends under the parson's nose and knot together. Cut off the excess string.

Once it is trussed, spread the top of the bird with softened butter and season generously with salt and pepper. A few rashers (strips) of streaky (fatty) bacon can be arraned over the breast area to stop the meat drying out. Roast following the times and temperatures on page 44.

succulent roast chicken

A well-flavoured stuffing packed under the skin of a whole chicken helps to keep the breast meat moist and succulent while it cooks. The flavour seeps right into the chicken so even the gravy picks up a hint of it. The stuffing should contain a little fat, diced bacon or chorizo, as well as other strong flavours such as capers, anchovies, herbs, chillies and other spices.

Serves 4–5

150 g (5½ oz) soft spreadable goat's cheese

3 garlic cloves, crushed

small handful of mixed herbs (parsley, chervil, chives, rosemary, fennel), finely chopped

2 tablespoons capers, rinsed and chopped

salt and freshly ground black pepper

1 large chicken, about 1.8 kg (4 lb)

50 g (2 oz) butter, softened

200 ml (7 fl oz) dry white wine or chicken stock

Preheat the oven to 220°C/425°F/Gas mark 7. Put the goat's cheese in a small bowl and beat in the garlic, herbs, capers, a little salt and plenty of pepper.

Carefully slide your fingers between the skin and breast meat of the chicken to release the skin. Work your fingers over the tops of the chicken legs as far as you can reach, taking care not to break the skin. Use a teaspoon to pack the stuffing between the skin and meat, spreading it as far as you can over the breast and leg meat. Ease the skin back into place and ensure the stuffing is spread in an even layer.

Truss the chicken, weigh and calculate the cooking time. Place in a roasting tin (pan) and spread with the butter. Roast for 20 minutes then reduce the cooking temperature to 180°C/350°F/Gas mark 4 and roast for the calculated time, basting with the pan juices several times during cooking.

Test that the chicken is cooked (see page 43), and transfer to a carving platter or board. Cover with foil and leave to rest in a warm place for 20–30 minutes.

To make the gravy, drain off the excess fat from the roasting tin and place over a gentle heat. Add a dash of wine or stock and stir well, scraping up the sediment. Blend in the remaining wine or stock and keep stirring until the gravy is thickened and bubbling. Season to taste.

roast turkey with chorizo and sweet potato stuffing

When calculating the size turkey to buy, allow about 300 g (10½ oz) per person, or 500 g (1 lb 2 oz) if you want leftovers. Pack the stuffing into the neck cavity only to ensure it cooks and shape the remainder into small balls for roasting separately. This is delicious with classic roast potatoes or for a change, try a spicy rice accompaniment.

Serves 8–12

125 g (4½ oz) butter

1 onion, chopped

2 celery sticks, chopped

1 medium-hot red chilli, deseeded and chopped

500 g (1 lb 2 oz) chorizo sausage, finely diced

300 g (10½ oz) sweet potato, scrubbed and
    coarsely grated

4 tablespoons chopped oregano

4 tablespoons chopped parsley

salt

1 turkey, about 5 kg (11 lb)

2 tablespoons plain (all-purpose) flour

600 ml (1 pint) chicken stock

To make the stuffing, melt the butter in a frying pan and gently soften the onion and celery for 5 minutes, stirring frequently. Stir in the chilli and chorizo and fry for another 2 minutes. Remove from the heat and tip into a bowl. Add the sweet potato, herbs and a sprinkling of salt and mix well. Leave to cool.

Preheat the oven to 220°C/425°F/Gas mark 7. Prepare the turkey for roasting and pack some of the stuffing into the neck cavity of the bird. Tuck the flap of skin under the stuffing to hold it in place. Weigh the bird to calculate the cooking time and place in a roasting tin (pan). Roast for 30 minutes then reduce the oven temperature to 180°C/350°F/Gas mark 4 and roast for the calculated time, basting the bird with the pan juices and covering with foil if it starts to over-brown.

Meanwhile, take dessertspoonfuls of the remaining stuffing and shape it into small balls. Add to the roasting tin 40 minutes before the end of the calculated cooking time.

Test that the turkey is cooked and transfer to a carving platter or board along with the stuffing balls. Cover with foil and leave to rest in a warm place for 20–30 minutes.

To make the gravy, drain off the excess fat from the roasting tin. Place the tin over a gentle heat, add the flour and stir well, scraping up the pan juices and meat residue. Gradually blend in the stock and keep stirring until the gravy is slightly thickened and bubbling. Season to taste and strain through a sieve into a gravy boat.

roast partridge with celeriac mash

Partridge is a good choice if you've not cooked small game birds before. It is fairly mild in flavour and plump so it roasts well and is easy to serve, one per portion. The trick is to keep the birds moist and succulent b blanketing them in fat bacon or butter and to avoid over cooking. Use a good shicken stock for the gravy as it'll have plenty of flavour when it's reduced. Partridge is only available for a few months of the year so make the most of it when you see it.

Serves 4

4 partridges
salt and freshly ground black pepper
25 g (1 oz) butter, softened
pinch each of ground cloves and nutmeg
8 rashers (strips) of streaky (fatty) bacon
300 ml (½ pint) chicken stock
2 tablespoons redcurrant, quince or crab apple jelly
    (jam), plus extra to serve
watercress, to garnish

FOR THE CELERIAC MASH
1 large celeriac, about 900 g (2 lb)
1 large potato
75 ml (5 tablespoons) single (light) cream
25 g (1 oz) butter

Preheat the oven to 220°C/425°F/Gas mark 7. Wipe the partridges inside and out with kitchen paper and season with salt and pepper. Place in a small roasting tin (pan). Beat the butter with the cloves and nutmeg and spread over the top of each bird. Arrange the bacon slices over the birds, cutting the bacon to fit.

Roast for 30 minutes. While the birds are cooking put the chicken stock in a pan and bring to the boil. Boil rapidly until reduced by about a third.

For the celeriac purée, peel and cut the celeriac into small chunks. Cut the potato into similarly sized pieces and place both in a pan of cold water. Bring to the boil, add salt to the water, and boil for about 20 minutes until both vegetables are tender. Drain well, return to the saucepan and mash thoroughly with the cream, butter and plenty of black pepper.

Remove the partridges from the oven and test that they are cooked. Remove the birds from the roasting tin, cover with foil and keep warm while making the gravy. Pour the reduced chicken stock into the roasting tin, add the jelly and cook over the stove top, stirring to blend the cooking juices and melt the jelly. Once the gravy is smooth and bubbling, season to taste and strain through a sieve into a small jug (pitcher) or gravy boat. Place the partridges on warmed serving plates with the celeriac mash and a pile of watercress. Pour over a little gravy.

blackened duck with flatbreads and lime yogurt

This recipe demonstrates how you can slow roast meat by coating the skin in a thick, well-flavoured baste that seeps right into the flesh. Like lamb and pork, duck is fatty enough to be cooked gently and slowly until the meat just falls off the bone. A roasted duck really only serves three people so to serve six you'll need to cook two ducks side by side. Unlike other slow roasts, you can't go away and forget about this one since it needs continual basting with the spicy juices during cooking.

Serves 6

2 hot green chillies, deseeded and
    roughly chopped
100 g (3½ oz) fresh root ginger, roughly chopped
4 garlic cloves, roughly chopped
6 tablespoons dark muscovado (molasses) sugar
90 ml (6 tablespoons) soy sauce
2 whole ducks, each weighing
    about 1.5 kg (3 lb 5 oz)

FOR THE LIME YOGURT
200 ml (7 fl oz) Greek (strained plain) yogurt
1 garlic clove, crushed
finely grated zest of 2 limes, plus 30 ml
    (2 tablespoons) juice

TO SERVE
12 warmed flatbreads
2 spring onions (scallions)
2 small cucumbers, cut into matchsticks
25 g (1 oz) fresh coriander (cilantro),
    roughly chopped
15 ml (1 tablespoon) rice wine or
    white wine vinegar
30 ml (2 tablespoons) ground nut or
    vegetable oil

Preheat the oven to 220°C/425°F/Gas mark 7. Put the chillies, ginger, garlic, sugar and soy sauce in a food processor or blender and blend to a loose paste. Alternatively, finely chop the chillies, ginger and garlic and mix with the sugar and soy sauce.

Pull out any pieces of loose fat from inside the cavity and reserve. Turn the birds over and prick all over the undersides and the legs with the tip of a skewer. This enables the fat to seep out during roasting. Turn the ducks the right way up and place on a rack over the kitchen sink. Pour a kettle full of boiling water all over the skin to open out the pores and help the skin to crisp up during cooking. Pat dry with kitchen paper.

Rest the racks holding the ducks on a roasting tin (pan). Roast for 30 minutes then reduce the oven temperature to 140°C/275°F/Gas mark 1. Lift the ducks off the racks and drain off the fat from the tin. Return the ducks to the rack and spoon over the chilli mixture.

Roast for 3½ hours, basting hourly with the pan juices. To do this lift the racks off the roasting tin and pour the juices into a small bowl. Return the racks to the tin and spoon over the glaze.

While roasting, mix together the yogurt, garlic and lime zest and juice and put in a serving dish. Peel the cucumber and cut into thin sticks. Finely chop the spring onions. Mix with the coriander and cucumber and put in a serving dish. Beat together the vinegar and oil and drizzle over the salad just before serving.

Remove the ducks from the oven and transfer to a board. Wrap the flatbreads in foil and heat through in the oven for 10 minutes.

Remove the legs from the ducks and place on a large warmed serving platter. Remove the duckbreasts from the carcass and cut these across into slices before adding to the platter. Serve with the flatbreads and salad.

pot-roasted pheasant

Pot roasting is brilliant for pheasant and other game birds as these have a tendency towards dryness, which is counteracted by the cooking juices and low oven temperatures. Serve with creamy mashed potatoes and seasonal vegetables.

Serves 4–5

25 g (1 oz) mixed dried mushrooms

2 pheasants, prepared

salt and freshly ground black pepper

100 g (3½ oz) smoked streaky (fatty) bacon

40 g (1½ oz) butter

15 ml (1 tablespoon) vegetable oil

2 small onions, chopped

2 garlic cloves, crushed

1 tablespoon plain (all-purpose) flour

300 ml (½ pint) red wine

10 juniper berries

2 tablespoons bramble or blackberry jelly

Preheat the oven to 150°C/300°F/Gas mark 2. Put the dried mushrooms in a small heatproof bowl and add 300 ml (10 fl oz) boiling water. Leave to stand for 15 minutes. Sprinkle the pheasants with salt and pepper. Chop the bacon into very small dice.

Melt the butter with the vegetable oil in a frying pan. Add the pheasants, one at a time and sear until golden, turning each bird as each area is browned. Transfer to a large casserole dish or deep-sided roasting tin (pan).

Add the bacon and onions to the frying pan and fry gently until just beginning to colour, adding the garlic for the last minute or so. Sprinkle in the flour and cook stirring for 1 minute. Remove from the heat and gradually blend in the red wine until no lumps of flour remain. Crush the juniper berries using a pestle and mortar or a small bowl and the end of a rolling pin. Return the frying pan to the heat and add the juniper berries, the mushrooms and their soaking liquid, and the bramble or blackberry jelly. Bring to the boil. Remove from the heat and tip the contents of the pan over the pheasants. Cover with a lid and transfer to the oven. Cook for 1½–2 hours or until very tender. The juices should run clear when the thickest part of the thigh is pierced with a skewer. Check the seasoning of the gravy and serve.

Frying

Most meat is fried at some point during the cooking process, either to give a deliciously caramelized surface prior to cooking or to cook it through completely. If you are stewing, casseroling or pot roasting, frying meat properly brings out its natural sweetness and gives the finished dish its rich burnished colour. Done properly, frying takes you halfway to a successful meal. Shallow frying is a quick and easy cooking method for prime tender steaks and is one of the fastest ways to knock up a tasty meal. Deep frying produces the kind of food we all love (but shouldn't eat too often!) with delicious results that are crispy and crunchy on the outside and moist and tender inside. Stir-frying is a brilliant choice for quick and easy meals that give us a good balance of meat and vegetables in one pan.

The type of fat used for frying is important as each has a different 'smoking point' – the temperature at which it starts to smoke and break down. If heated any further than this, the fat is likely to burn, turn bitter and taint the flavour of the finished dish. Vegetable oils such as groundnut, corn and sunflower have the highest smoking point and the least flavour. They are good for browning meats, deep frying and stir-frying. 'Stir-fry' or 'wok' oils are usually groundnut oil flavoured with aromatic ingredients such as garlic and ginger that contribute to the flavour of Asian stir-fries. Duck, goose and bacon fat provide a distinctive flavour and richness but will overheat more quickly than vegetable oil. Olive oil is also used for shallow and deep frying but use a mild, less expensive one, keeping your best for sauces and dressings. Butter has the lowest smoking point but plenty of flavour so it's sometimes combined with vegetable oil for shallow frying to reduce the risk of burning.

Frying tips

- Frying is infinitely more enjoyable if you have a decent pan, whether you're using a frying pan, wok, ridged pan or deep fryer. You might be able to get away with a cheap wok but it's definitely worth buying a good-quality frying pan, if you intend to fry a lot of food. They are expensive but will last for years if used properly.
- Always heat the pan before adding the oil or fat. This will get it hot quickly and ultimately make your pan last longer.
- Make sure meats are thoroughly dry before frying. Moisture will cause spluttering and the meat will cook in steam created by the moisture, rather than fry.
- Shallow frying is a very quick cooking process. Thin pieces of meat such as escalopes will cook quicker than you think. Take care not to overdo it or the texture of the meat will start to toughen.
- Have all your preparation done before frying. Accompaniments should be ready before you start shallow or deep frying and ingredients chopped and ready for stir-frying.

- Wooden tongs, or a flat-edged wooden spoon or spatula, are good for turning meat so you don't damage the pan.
- Meat fried at room temperature will cook through slightly more quickly than if cooked straight from the refrigerator.
- When shallow frying avoid the temptation to keep turning the meat as it browns. You'll get a better colour if you let one side brown completely before flipping it over. In contrast, stir-fried ingredients should be kept constantly on the move as you cook them.

Browning meat

For stews, casseroles and hot pots, thoroughly browning or 'searing' the meat is a vital part of developing flavour and providing a good, rich colour. Trim, dice or roll the meat according to your chosen recipe and make sure it's really dry, if necessary patting with kitchen paper to remove any surface moisture. Toss the meat in seasoned flour if the recipe requires. This gives a good colour and will help thicken the cooking juices of stews and casseroles.

Heat the frying pan or large flameproof casserole dish. Once hot, add a little oil, or chosen fat. Add the meat once the fat is melted or the oil is hot. It's easy to tell when oil is hot as its consistency thins. Make sure the pieces of meat have plenty of space around them in the pan – if close together or touching they'll steam rather than fry. Leave for a minute or two until the underside of the meat has browned, then turn it so all sides of the meat become evenly browned. When the meat is a deep, rich caramel colour, drain it with a slotted spoon and fry the remainder in batches. Use the same method for joints of meat, turning the meat slowly so all the surfaces, including the ends, are browned.

Shallow frying

Meats that are cooked by shallow frying need fast-cooking cuts (see page 15). Cooking times depend on the thickness of the meat used and the frying temperature. Have the pan hot before adding the fat or oil and then heat the oil before adding the meat. Once seared on all sides at the necessary high temperature the heat can be reduced so the meat cooks through gently. Some shallow-fried dishes are finished by adding other ingredients such as a tomato or cream sauce, which soak up all the meaty pan juices.

Deep frying

The safest way to deep fry is to use an electric deep fryer with a thermostat, which automatically turns the appliance off if the oil gets too hot. You can also use a sturdy deep-frying pan that comes with a frying basket or a regular large saucepan. In either case, take great care with deep frying as over-heated oil can be very dangerous. Fill the pan no more than a third full with oil. Never leave the pan unattended and if possible use a thermometer to keep an eye on the temperature. For most deep-fried meat dishes, the temperature should be 190°C (375°F), or until a piece of bread sizzles and turns golden in 1 minute. A safer and more controllable way of deep frying is to use a large, wide pan or a frying pan with deep sides and fill it with just 2 cm (¾ in) of oil. This is perfect for thin slices or small chunks of meat such as the Crispy Chicken Nuggets with Tomato Dip on page 104.

Stir-frying

Woks are ideal for stir-frying as the sloping sides give a maximum surface area for fast cooking. You only need about a tablespoon of oil as the ingredients get hot very quickly and are constantly turned with a large heatproof spatula or spoon. Have all the ingredients, including dressings, sauces and flavourings chopped and ready before you start. Both meat and vegetables should be cut into small even-sized pieces so they cook quickly. Use fast-cooking cuts of meat and slice them across the grain for tender results.

There are four basic steps to a simple stir-fry. First the aromatic flavourings such as shallots, garlic, chilli and ginger are cooked briefly in the hot oil to release their flavour. These are then removed and the meat is added to the flavoured oil and tossed around in the pan before removing. The vegetables are added next, starting with the ones that take the longest to cook such as carrots and celery, gradually adding softer, quicker-cooking vegetables like courgettes (zucchini), mushrooms and spring onions (scallions). The ingredients should be kept on the move all the time. Finally, all the cooked ingredients are returned to the wok or pan along, with any herbs, sauces or dressings and noodles, to heat through and combine. You can easily knock up your own simple stir-fries using this basic method and any ingredients you have to hand, drizzling the finished stir-fry with soy or hoisin sauce.

How to fry the perfect steak

Perfectly cooked steak is beautifully seared on the outside and juicy and succulent inside. Fillet, sirloin, rump, T-bone and rib-eye steaks are all perfect for frying. Choose ones of even thickness, about 2 cm (¾ in) thick and trim off any loose fat. Season the steaks on both sides just before you start cooking and remember to have warmed plates and accompaniments ready and waiting.

Use a sturdy frying pan and heat a little butter with a dash of oil until the butter is melted and bubbling hot. Alternatively used a ridged pan.

Add the steak or steaks, leaving plenty of space between them. Once cooked for the required time on one side (see below), turn the steaks and cook for the remaining time before transfering to warmed serving plates.

Don't waste the delicious juices left in the pan after cooking. Add a splash of rich stock or red or white wine and stir with a wooden spoon to blend the meat residue with the liquid. Let the mixture bubble up and reduce slightly before adding any additional flavouring like a dollop of crème fraîche, splash of cream, scattering of herbs, capers, chopped gherkins, crushed green peppercorns or mustard. Check the seasoning before serving. Alternatively, you can simply drizzle the tasty pan juices over the steaks.

Cooking times for steak

For steaks of about 2 cm (¾ in) thickness use the following times as a guide:

- Blue: Cook for a few seconds on each side so the steak is seared on the outside but completely raw in the centre.
- Rare: Cook for 1½ minutes on each side or until there is a thin area of cooked meat but the centre is uncooked.
- Medium: Cook for 2½ minutes on each side or until most of the steak is cooked through but a thin band of pink remains in the centre.
- Well done: Cook for 5 minutes on each side or until there is no sign of any pinkness in the centre.

beefburgers

Once you have made your own burgers you will never want to eat ready-made ones again. Use good-quality steak mince, season to your taste and add additional flavourings as you like. This recipe shows that burgers made using good-quality meat don't need any help from other ingredients.

Serves 4

750 g (1 lb 10 oz) good quality minced beef

salt and freshly ground black pepper

30 ml (2 tablespoons) vegetable oil

4 burger buns, split and buttered (or plain)

lettuce, tomato slices and finely sliced red onion

mayonnaise or mustard, or both, to serve

Tip the beef into a bowl and season well. Work the ingredients thoroughly together with your hands so you can make sure the seasoning is evenly dispersed through the meat. Divide the mixture into 4 evenly sized pieces and press each into a burger shape about 2 cm (¾ in) thick.

Pour the vegetable oil into a heated frying pan. Once the oil is hot, add the burgers and fry, turning once, until golden brown on each side and cooked to your liking. As a guide allow 2–3 minutes each side for a medium-rare burger, 4 minutes each side for medium burger and 5–6 minutes each side for well done.

Pack a little lettuce, tomato and onion into the burger buns. Top with the burgers, mayonnaise and mustard, and serve.

Variations
• For lamb burgers: use good quality lamb instead of beef and add flavourings such as a chopped mint or coriander. A little crushed garlic and a generous pinch of allspice or cinnamon is also good.
• For porkburgers: use good quality minced pork instead of beef and add a little mustard, a sprinkling of paprika, finely chopped sage, thyme, or chilli.

veal escalopes with dill and caper sauce

Use ready-prepared escalopes for this recipe, or buy a piece of veal topside or rump and cut it into escalopes (see page 33). The recipe works equally well with pork escalopes or chicken breast, bashed thin. This dish cooks quickly so have the accompaniments such as creamy mash and seasonal green vegetables prepared before you start frying.

Serves 4

2 teaspoons plain (all-purpose) flour

salt and freshly ground black pepper

4 x 150 g (5½ oz) veal escalopes

50 g (2 oz) butter

250 ml (9 fl oz) dry white wine

2 tablespoons chopped dill

1 tablespoon capers, rinsed and drained

Put the flour on a plate and season well with salt and pepper. Turn the escalopes in the flour until lightly coated on both sides.

Melt half the butter in a large frying pan until bubbling hot, making sure it doesn't start to brown around the edges. Add the veal escalopes, two at a time if the pan is not large enough to take them all in one go. Fry for 1½–2 minutes on each side or until pale golden. Drain to a plate and keep warm.

Pour the wine into the frying pan, bring to the boil and let it bubble until reduced by about half and slightly thickened. Add the dill and capers and dot in the remaining butter. Turn off the heat and use a balloon whisk to beat the sauce ingredients together until the butter melts and the sauce is slightly glossy. Check the seasoning for taste. Place the escalopes on warm serving plates and spoon over the sauce.

stir-fried beef
and noodles

This is a simple stir-fry recipe that makes a little steak go a long way, and is ideal for an easy supper.

Serves 4

400 g (14 oz) sirloin or rump steak

75 ml (5 tablespoons) dark soy sauce

½ teaspoon five-spice powder

200 g (7 oz) fine rice noodles

1 teaspoon cornflour (cornstarch)

1 tablespoon caster (superfine) sugar

30 ml (2 tablespoons) wok or vegetable oil

25 g (1 oz) fresh root ginger, peeled
   and finely chopped

1 hot red chilli, deseeded and thinly sliced

3 garlic cloves, thinly sliced

1 bunch spring onions (scallions), trimmed and cut
   into 2 cm (¾ in) lengths

200 g (7 oz) sugarsnap peas, sliced thinly
   lengthways

Trim off any fat from the steak and cut across into 5 mm (¼ in) thick slices. If the slices are long, cut them into 5cm (2 in) lengths. Mix 15 ml (1 tablespoon) of the soy sauce in a bowl with the five-spice powder. Add the meat and mix well until evenly coated. Leave to marinate while preparing the other ingredients.

Cook the noodles following the packet directions. Drain. Mix the cornflour with 30 ml (2 tablespoons) water in a small bowl. To this add the remaining soy sauce and the sugar.

Heat half the oil in a wok or large frying pan. Add the ginger, chilli and garlic, and fry, stirring for 30 seconds. Drain to a plate with a slotted spoon.

Add the beef to the pan and stir-fry for 1½ minutes until browned. Drain to the plate. Heat the remaining oil in the pan, add the spring onions and sugar snaps and stir-fry for 2 minutes. Once the vegetables have softened slightly, return the meat to the pan with the noodles and soy sauce mixture. Cook for 1 minute or until heated through, mixing the ingredients together.

frying

calves' liver and bacon with onion chutney

Calves' liver is the most tender and delicate of all the livers. It is also great for frying and some prefer it for its richer flavour. In this recipe the bacon is fried first to flavour the pan juices before frying the liver.

Serves 4

700 g (1 lb 9 oz) calves' liver, sliced

salt and freshly ground black pepper

15 g (½ oz) butter

15 ml (1 tablespoon) vegetable or mild olive oil

8 rashers (strips) smoked back bacon

FOR THE ONION CHUTNEY

30 ml (2 tablespoons) vegetable or mild olive oil

325 g (11½ oz) red onions, thinly sliced

2 tablespoons dark muscovado (molasses) sugar

1 teaspoon chopped thyme

45 ml (3 tablespoons) balsamic vinegar

To make the chutney, heat the vegetable oil in a saucepan or frying pan. Add the onions and fry gently for about 6–8 minutes, stirring frequently, until the onions are soft and beginning to colour. Continue to cook the onions until they start to turn deep golden and caramelized. Stir in the sugar, thyme, vinegar and 60 ml (4 tablespoons) water and cook gently for another 5–10 minutes or until the onions are very soft and the juices slightly glossy. Remove from the heat.

Cut away any tubes from the liver and season on both sides with salt and pepper. Melt the butter with the oil in a large, hot frying pan until the butter starts to bubble up. Add the bacon and fry on both sides for about 5 minutes, until golden and beginning to crisp. Lift the bacon out of the pan and keep warm.

Add the liver to the pan and fry for 2 minutes or until golden on the underside. Turn the pieces over and fry for another minute (at this stage the liver will be slightly pink in the centre so cook for another 1–2 minutes if you prefer it cooked through).

Transfer the liver to warmed serving plates and place the bacon on top. Drizzle with the pan juices and serve topped with the onion chutney.

italian meatballs with tomato sauce

Meatballs are one of the great comfort foods, each morsel packed with flavour. Serve on a bed of pasta, creamy polenta, rice or simply with chunks of warmed, crusty bread.

Serves 4

500 g (1 lb 2 oz) lean minced beef

2 small red onions, finely chopped

25 g (1 oz) breadcrumbs

50 g (2 oz) Parmesan cheese, grated

2 tablespoons chopped oregano

salt and freshly ground black pepper

60 ml (4 tablespoons) olive oil

2 garlic cloves, crushed

150 ml (5 fl oz) red wine

800 g (1 lb 12 oz) canned plum tomatoes

2 teaspoons light muscovado (brown) sugar

2 tablespoons sun-dried tomato purée (paste)

small handful of pitted black olives

Put the mince in a bowl and add half the chopped onion, the breadcrumbs, Parmesan, oregano and a little salt and pepper. Using your hands, mix the ingredients together until evenly combined. Scoop up small pieces of the mixture and shape into balls, about 2.5 cm (1 in) in diameter.

Heat half the oil in a large frying pan. Add the meatballs and cook, shaking the pan frequently and turning the meatballs until they're golden on all sides. Drain to a plate.

Add the remaining oil and onion to the pan and fry gently, stirring for 5 minutes and adding the garlic for the last minute. Pour in the wine and bring to the boil. Boil rapidly until the wine has reduced by about half. Stir in the tomatoes, sugar, tomato purée and a little seasoning and bring to the boil. Cook quickly for about 5 minutes, breaking up the tomatoes with the edge of a wooden spoon so the sauce starts to thicken and turn pulpy.

Return the meatballs to the pan and scatter with the olives. Cook very gently for another 10 minutes. Season to taste and serve.

pork fillet with preserved lemon and crème fraîche

Tender pork fillet makes an easy and economical choice for a quick and simple supper dish. The preserved lemons add a tangy contrast and slightly exotic flavour. Serve with couscous or new potatoes.

Serves 2

400 g (14 oz) pork fillet

½ teaspoon ground cumin

½ teaspoon hot paprika

good pinch ground cinnamon

salt and freshly ground black pepper

1 preserved lemon from a jar, drained

1 garlic clove, finely chopped

3 tablespoons chopped parsley

25 g (1 oz) butter

50 ml (2 fl oz) crème fraîche

Cut the pork fillet across into 1 cm (½ in) slices. Mix together the cumin, paprika, cinnamon and a little salt. Sprinkle over the pork and rub in with your fingers.

Halve the lemon, scoop out and discard the pulp. Finely chop the peel and mix with the garlic and parsley.

Melt the butter in a frying pan. When hot and bubbling but not browned, add the pork, spacing the pieces slightly apart. Fry gently for 5 minutes, shaking the pan frequently. Turn the slices over and cook for another 2–3 minutes or until cooked through. Test by slicing through one piece – there should be no sign of pink.

Add the crème fraîche and 4 tablespoons water and stir until heated through and bubbling. Check the seasoning. Scatter with the lemon mixture and serve.

venison stroganoff

The secret of a successful stroganoff is to sear the meat very quickly before adding the sauce ingredients, then cook this quickly too as the meat will go on cooking and you don't want it to toughen. Have accompaniments such as buttery rice and a rocket salad ready on the table and serve the stroganoff straight from the pan. Beef fillet can be used instead for a more traditional version.

Serves 4

800 g (1 lb 12 oz) piece venison loin or fillet

1 teaspoon freshly ground black pepper

salt

50 g (2 oz) butter

15 m (1 tablespoon) vegetable oil

2 onions, thinly sliced

300 g (11 oz) chestnut mushrooms, thinly sliced

200 ml (7 fl oz) crème fraîche

4 tablespoons finely chopped parsley

Cut the venison across the grain into 1.5 cm (⅝ in) thick slices. Cut these slices across into 1.5 cm (⅝ in) thick strips. If the strips are long cut them down to about 5 cm (2 in) lengths. Place in a bowl and sprinkle with the pepper and a little salt. Toss the meat in the seasoning.

Put half the butter and half the oil in a large frying pan and heat until the butter is bubbling. Add the onions and fry gently for 5 minutes, stirring until softened but not browned. Add the mushrooms and fry for another couple of minutes until softened. Tip out onto a plate.

Heat the remaining butter and oil in the pan. Once bubbling add the venison and fry quickly, turning the meat until golden on all sides. Return the onions and mushrooms to the pan along with the crème fraîche and 30 ml (2 tablespoons) water. Cook quickly, stirring well to combine the ingredients. Sprinkle with parsley and serve.

spiced pigeon pilaf

There's a Moroccan pie recipe called Bisteeya in which a spicy pigeon and dried fruit filling is wrapped in pastry, dusted with icing sugar and branded with a heated skewer. If that all sounds a little extreme, this recipe, using some of the above ingredients, should have more universal appeal.

Serves 4

50 g (2 oz) flaked (slivered) almonds

8 pigeon breasts

salt and freshly ground black pepper

75 ml (5 tablespoons) olive oil

2 onions, chopped

3 garlic cloves, thinly sliced

25 g (1 oz) fresh root ginger, finely chopped

2 teaspoons cumin seeds, crushed

1 teaspoon ground cinnamon

250 g (9 oz) long grain rice

500 ml (18 fl oz) chicken or vegetable stock

1 teaspoon saffron strands

4 tablespoons chopped parsley

4 tablespoons chopped fresh coriander (cilantro)

Heat a large frying pan. Scatter in the almonds and lightly toast them, shaking the pan and turning the almonds until they're lightly browned. Tip out onto a plate.

Cut the pigeon breasts into 5 mm (¼ in) thick slices and season lightly. Heat 15 ml (1 tablespoon) of the oil in the pan. Add the pigeon pieces and fry quickly for 1½–2 minutes, turning the pieces frequently until browned but still pink in the centre. Turn out onto the plate.

Add the remaining oil to the pan and gently fry the onions for 5 minutes until softened. Stir in the garlic, ginger, cumin, cinnamon and rice and stir for another minute, turning the rice until coated in the spices.

Add the stock and crumble in the saffron. Bring to the boil and reduce the heat to its lowest setting. Cover with a lid or foil and cook gently for about 20 minutes, checking several times that the rice hasn't dried out. If necessary, stir in a little boiling water.

Once the rice is tender, return the pigeon to the pan along with the almonds, parsley and coriander. Season to taste and heat through for a couple of minutes before serving.

easy chicken liver pâté

Chicken livers make a lovely light pâté that can be whizzed up in the food processor. The more you blend the lighter and creamier the pâté becomes. It is then sealed in melted butter, which keeps it fresh for several days in the refrigerator. Serve with warmed bread or toast, pickled onions, gherkins or onion chutney.

Serves 6

500 g (1 lb 2 oz) fresh chicken livers

150 g (5½ oz) butter

1 onion, roughly chopped

1 tablespoon lemon thyme leaves

30 ml (2 tablespoons) brandy

1 tablespoon green peppercorns in brine, rinsed and drained

salt

Rinse the chicken livers and pat dry on kitchen paper. Halve the livers and snip out the white parts using scissors (no need to do this too thoroughly).

Put half of the butter in a small saucepan, heat gently until it has melted. Slowly pour the melted butter into a small jug (pitcher), leaving the white sediment that will have separated out of the butter in the saucepan. Set aside

Melt another 25g (1 oz) of the butter in a frying pan. Add the onion and half the thyme leaves and fry gently for 2 minutes. Add the chicken livers and fry for another 4 minutes or until plumped up and still slightly pink in the centre. Add the brandy and cook briefly.

Tip the chicken livers and cooking juices into a food processor and blend until smooth, scraping down any pieces that cling to the sides of the bowl. Once the mixture is smooth add a small piece of the remaining butter and whizz until melted. Continue to add the remaining butter, piece by piece until smooth.

Transfer the pâté to a serving dish or individual ramekins and pat down with the back of a spoon. Carefully spoon the melted butter over the top. Lightly crush the peppercorns and scatter over the top with the remaining thyme leaves. Chill for several hours until the butter has set before serving.

crispy chicken nuggets with tomato dip

Homemade chicken nuggets are so easy to make and once you've tried them you'll never buy frozen ones again. Serve with chunky chips and a leafy salad.

Serves 4

4 skinless chicken breasts

2 tablespoons plain (all-purpose) flour

salt and freshly ground black pepper

1 egg

½ teaspoon dried oregano

150 g (5½ oz) breadcrumbs

vegetable oil, for deep frying

FOR THE TOMATO DIP

100 ml (3½ fl oz) passatta

good pinch cayenne pepper

3 tablespoons light muscovado (brown) sugar

30 ml (2 tablespoons) red or white wine vinegar

Cut each chicken breast across into 5 mm (¼ in) thick slices. Sprinkle the flour onto a plate and add a little salt and pepper. Mix together. Break the egg onto a second plate and beat with a fork to break it up. Mix the oregano and breadcrumbs together on a third plate.

Lightly dust each piece of chicken in seasoned flour then dip it in the egg. Let the excess drip off and then roll each in the breadcrumbs until coated.

To make the dip, put the passata, pepper, sugar, vinegar and a pinch of salt in a bowl and whisk to combine. Turn into a small serving bowl.

Heat 1.5 cm (¾ in) depth of oil in a deep-sided frying pan or wide shallow saucepan until the temperature reaches 190°C (375°F), or until a cube of bread sizzles and turns golden in 1 minute. Once the temperature is reached turn down the heat slightly. Add several pieces of the chicken and fry gently, turning the chicken with a metal spoon until golden. Using a slotted spoon, drain the chicken to a plate lined with kitchen paper and cook the remainder in the same way. Serve with the tomato dip.

sticky chicken with chilli crumbs

Chicken thighs have a rich flavour that are complemented by the fried breadcrumb coating. The crumbs in this recipe are spiced with chilli, but you can leave this ingredient out, if you prefer.

Serves 4

100 g (3½ oz) firm stale bread such as ciabatta

75 ml (5 tablespoons) olive oil

1 medium-hot red chilli, finely chopped

2 garlic cloves, finely chopped

4 tablespoons chopped fresh coriander (cilantro)

salt

8 skinned and boned chicken thighs, thinly sliced

1 red onion, thinly sliced

2 large courgettes (zucchini), cut into matchsticks

4 red (bell) peppers or mixed (bell) peppers, deseeded and thinly sliced

FOR THE GLAZE

1 teaspoon cornflour (cornstarch)

90 ml (6 tablespoons) orange juice

30 ml (2 tablespoons) clear honey

30 ml (2 tablespoons) tomato puree

30 ml (2 tablespoons) Worcestershire sauce

Tear the bread into pieces slightly bigger than coarse breadcrumbs. Heat 45 ml (3 tablespoons) of the oil in frying pan. Add the bread and chilli and fry gently for 2–3 minutes. Add the garlic, coriander and salt and cook for another 1–2 minutes. Tip out onto a plate.

For the glaze, put the cornflour in a small bowl and gradually blend in the orange juice then the honey, tomato purée and Worcestershire sauce.

Heat a dash more oil. Stir-fry the chicken in batches, transferring each batch to a plate once cooked. This should take about 4 minutes per batch. Heat a little more oil and add the onion and courgettes. Stir-fry for 3–4 minutes until beginning to colour. Drain to the plate with the chicken. Heat the remaining oil and stir-fry the peppers for 8–10 minutes until softened and beginning to colour.

Return the chicken and cooked vegetables to the pan along with the glaze. Cook, stirring for a couple of minutes until the chicken is hot and coated in the glaze.

Spoon onto warmed serving plates and scatter with the crumbs.

Grilling and Barbecuing

These are fast ways of cooking meat and only suitable for prime tender cuts. Meat can either be cooked under a conventional grill (broiler), on the grid of a barbecue, or in a ridged pan over the stove top. The heat is dry and intense so take care to avoid over-cooking and losing the juicy succulence of the meat. Any surface or integral fat in the meat helps to baste it naturally, but you can also keep meat moist by marinating it or basting it with oils and butters as it cooks.

Grilling and barbecuing tips

• Make sure the grill or pan is preheated before adding the meat so it sears quickly, retaining all its flavour and juices. If using a barbecue the flames should have died down and the coals be gently glowing before adding any meat. Once the meat is cooked on the outside you can always turn the heat down (or transfer the meat to a less hot area of the barbecue) if the centre isn't cooked enough for your taste.

• Brush the surface of very lean meats with oil before cooking rather than the grill rack or barbecue rack. This will help prevent sticking or flare ups if barbecuing.

• Meat should be of equal thickness so that it all cooks at the same rate. Poussin and small game birds can be 'spatchcocked' (see page 112), so they cook through evenly.

• Marinades and rubs are great for adding flavour prior to cooking. You can also baste meat with flavoured oils as it cooks. When making marinades and rubs, don't add salt as it draws out the juices from the meat. Add salt immediately before or during cooking.

• If using an overhead grill, line the grill pan with a sheet of foil each time you cook. This makes the pan easier to clean and helps prevent a build-up of charred grease and fat.

• Use tongs, rather than forks to turn meats so the skin is not pierced. A pastry brush is ideal for basting.

• Some range-style stove tops have a flat, cast-iron hot plate. These can be used equally well for cooking kebabs, burgers and small pieces of meat. Use them in the same way that you'd use the ridged pan.

• This is a fast way of cooking meat so the rules about 'resting' meat apply (see page 45). However, as barbecues tend to be relaxed affairs, by the time everyone's organised with their drinks and accompaniments, the meat is usually rested anyway.

Using a ridged pan

Ridged grill pans are used on the stove top but create the effect of barbecuing as the meat is seared with lightly charred lines. They take longer to heat than a regular frying pan and must be very hot before adding the meat or you run the risk of it sticking. Brush the meat with oil before adding to the pan and let it cook completely on the underside, undisturbed, before turning it. If you keep moving the meat you won't end up with well-defined lines. To see whether the meat is cooked on the underside, carefully lift the corner of one piece before turning the whole piece. If it needs longer, put the meat back down in the same position. Cooking times for chargrilling this way are much the same as for frying.

Using a barbecue

Badly barbecued meat is black on the outside and raw in the centre. This happens when the meat is added to the rack before the flames have died down sufficiently. Aim for the coals to be gently glowing before you put the meat on, so make sure you leave plenty of time, usually about 20–30 minutes before you even think about cooking. It's best to use natural lumpwood charcoal rather than the fuel-injected briquesttes which can create a very intense heat and are harder to control. Once you've started cooking, the temperature can be adjusted by lifting the cooking rack higher or moving the food to the side of the barbecue where the heat might not be as intense. If fat drips down onto the coals and causes a flare up use a squirt of water to douse the flames. It's worth getting a spray bottle, such as those sold at garden centres or used as a laundry spray and filing it with water – just in case.

Making kebabs

Kebabs are great for grilling and barbecuing as it's much easier to turn skewers than small pieces of meat. Use metal skewers of a length that suits your portion sizes or bamboo skewers that you've first soaked in cold water for 30 minutes before threading so they don't burn during cooking. You can also wrap the skewers in pieces of foil. When threading kebabs, don't pack them too tightly onto the skewers, a little space between each will help heat circulation and the meat will cook faster. Don't forget to leave enough space at one end to provide a handle. Kebabs are a good way of cooking various different ingredients at the same time, but make sure they all have similar cooking times.

Bastes, marinades, rubs and butters

Use these to add extra flavour to grilled (broiled) meats. Bastes are usually oil or melted butter flavoured with ingredients such as crushed garlic, chopped herbs or crushed spices. Put several glugs of olive oil in a bowl, add a couple of crushed garlic cloves and plenty of salt and pepper, then any flavourings you choose. Herbs such as chopped parsley, chives, tarragon, dill, oregano, lovage and coriander can be used alone or combined. A finely crushed chilli will add heat, while crushed coriander, cumin, fennel or cardamom will add a warm spiciness. It's fun to experiment and you can't go wrong!

Simple marinades like those on page 34 can be used to add extra flavour to meats before grilling (broiling). After marinating, remember to drain off the excess and pat the meat dry on kitchen paper.

Herb or spice rubs can be spread over meat before grilling, but if the meat is particularly lean –such as chicken breasts or steak – you'll need to baste the surface with oil as it grills.

Flavoured butters make delicious toppings for grilled and barbecued meats. Spooned onto the meat once plated, the butter melts to create a delicious flavoured sauce. Try the one on page 118 or devise your own by adding ingredients such as finely chopped herbs, capers, gherkins, crushed spices, toasted nuts, horseradish, citrus zest, spring onions (scallions) or finely chopped shallots to seasoned softened butter.

How to spatchcock a bird

'Spatchcocking' is the way in which a bird is opened out flat for grilling or barbecuing. It's ideal for small birds, including poussin, partridge and quail, allowing them to be cooked through quickly and evenly. You'll need a pair of poultry shears or a sturdy pair of kitchen scissors and some metal or bamboo skewers (two per bird).

Turn the bird over with the breast side face down. Use scissors to cut along one side of the backbone then the other to remove the backbone completely. Turn the bird over, breast side up, and bend the legs out. Flatten out the bird by pushing down on the breastbone with the heel of your hand.

Push a skewer diagonally through the bird so the skewer goes through one leg and out through the wing on the opposite side. Push a second skewer through the bird in the opposite direction. The skewers keep the bird flat during cooking and are easy to pull out afterwards.

How to butterfly a leg of lamb

Butterflying a whole leg of lamb is one of the easier butchering tasks and a satisfying one to master, though you can ask your butcher to do it. Unlike 'tunnel boning' where the bones are carefully removed so the meat retains its leg shape, butterflying only aims to remove the bones while retaining the meat in a single piece, so if you find it difficult to follow the steps below you can 'do your own thing' as long as you end up with one large piece of boneless meat. 'Butterfly' describes the way the meat is opened out like wings, making a flat joint that's perfect for grilling and barbecuing. Don't forget to keep the bones for making lamb stock.

1 Place the leg on a large board with the fleshiest side face down. Run your fingers down the length of the leg to locate the bony areas (there are three bones in total). Cut down one side of the bone at the thickest end of the joint with a boning knife or other sturdy, sharp knife. Use the tip of the knife to scrape away at the meat, pulling the bone away with the other hand once you can get a grip on it.

2 Continue to work the knife down the joint, keeping it as close to the bone as you can to prevent wastage. Use small cutting strokes so you can carefully reveal the bone, rather than cutting into the lean meat. It helps to use the tip of the knife, rather than the full length of the blade.

3 Work around the ball and socket joint (about two-thirds of the way down the joint) pulling the bone away from the meat with one hand and scraping around the bones with the knife in the other hand.

4 When you get to the narrow end of the joint cut through the sinews to release the bones completely.

5 Tidy up the meat by cutting away any sinews and tendons from the thin end and trimming off any loose or excessive areas of fat. There should be two very plump areas of lean meat on the joint. Make a vertical cut halfway through each so the meat can be opened out for even cooking.

butterflied leg of lamb with goat's cheese dressing

A beautiful piece of lamb is one of the best barbecue treats. A small leg will serve four while a large one will stretch to eight. If you have to resort to indoor cooking use the conventional grill (broiler), allow 15–20 minutes each side, and watch closely so that it doesn't burn. If necessary, you can always pop it in a moderate oven to finish it off to your taste.

Serves 8

3 tablespoons green peppercorns in brine, rinsed and drained

4 garlic cloves, crushed

finely grated zest and juice of 1 lemon

30 ml (2 tablespoons) clear honey

3 tablespoons chopped thyme

salt and freshly ground black pepper

1 large leg of lamb, butterflied (2.5 kg/5½ lb see page 113)

300 g (10½ oz) soft rindless goats' cheese

100 ml (3½ fl oz) Greek (strained plain) yogurt

3 tablespoons chopped chives

2 tablespoons chopped parsley

Lightly crush the green peppercorns using a pestle and mortar or a small bowl and the end of a rolling pin. Set one tablespoon aside and add the garlic, lemon zest and juice, honey, 30 ml (2 tablespoons) of the thyme and a little black pepper. Mix well and rub the marinade all over the lamb. Cover loosely and leave to marinate in a cool place for about 2 hours.

Put the goats' cheese and yogurt in a food processor and blend lightly to mix. Add the reserved green peppercorns, remaining thyme, chives, parsley and plenty of black pepper and blend again until mixed. Transfer to a serving bowl and chill until ready to serve.

Place the lamb on the prepared barbecue and cook for 15–20 minutes on each side or until crisp and browned on the outside. The meat will still be pink in the centre so cook for longer if you prefer it cooked through. Test by using a meat thermometer or by cutting into a thick area of the meat to see whether it's done to your taste.

Transfer to a carving board or platter, cover with foil and leave to stand for 15 minutes before serving.

harissa chicken, bulgar wheat and grapefruit salad

Grilled or barbecued – this salad makes delicious summer eating. Harissa is a hot and spicy North African paste that is added to meat and vegetable dishes. Use the rest from the jar to perk up soups and stews.

Serves 4

250 g (9 oz) bulgar wheat

1 tablespoon vegetable bouillon powder or
    1 crumbled vegetable stock cube

4 small chicken breasts

20 ml (4 teaspoons) harissa paste

125 ml (4 fl oz) olive oil

45 ml (3 tablespoons) clear honey

2 pink grapefruits

15 ml (1 tablespoon) lemon juice

1 pomegranate

1 small red onion, finely chopped

25 g (1 oz) parsley, finely chopped

Put the bulgar wheat in a saucepan with 1 litre (1¾ pints) boiling water and the bouillon powder or stock cube. Bring to the boil, reduce the heat to its lowest setting and cook gently for 5 minutes or until the bulgar wheat has softened and expanded. Drain and leave to cool.

Score the chicken breasts diagonally with a sharp knife, making the cuts about 2 cm (¾ in) apart. Place in a shallow, non-metallic dish. Mix the harissa paste with 10 ml (2 teaspoons) of the olive oil and 1 teaspoon of the honey. Tip over the chicken and turn the chicken in the paste until it is coated on all sides. Leave to marinate for about 30 minutes.

Tip the bulgar wheat into a bowl. Cut away the skin from the grapefruits. Working over a bowl to catch the juices, cut out the segments from between the membrane, adding the segments to the bulgar wheat. Mix 10 ml (2 tablespoons) of the grapefruit juice with the lemon juice, remaining olive oil, honey and seasoning.

Halve the pomegranate and separate the seeds, discarding the white membrane. Add the seeds to the bulgar wheat with the onion and parsley. Stir in the dressing. Season to taste.

Cook the chicken under a preheated grill (broiler), on the barbecue or in a ridged pan, allowing about 5 minutes each side. Cut into slices, scatter over the salad and serve.

pork chops with tomato and coriander butter

This simple recipe adds a contemporary twist to grilled pork chops by topping them with a tangy butter that melts deliciously all over the meat. Leftover butter keeps well in the refrigerator for several days and can be served with roast chicken, spread in sandwiches, or added to perk up a plain soup.

Serves 4

4 chunky pork loin chops

salt and freshly ground black pepper

140 g (5 oz) butter, softened

½ teaspoon ground coriander

½ teaspoon hot smoked paprika

dash of vegetable oil

50 g (2 oz) sun-dried tomatoes (drained of oil if from a jar), chopped

¼ teaspoon celery salt

2 tablespoons finely chopped fresh coriander (cilantro)

Season the pork chops on both sides with salt and pepper.

Melt 15 g (½ oz) of the butter in a small saucepan. Add the ground coriander and paprika and heat for 30 seconds. Remove from the heat and add the remaining butter. Mix well and stir in the tomatoes, celery salt, chopped coriander and a little pepper. Turn into a small serving dish.

Cook the pork chops under a preheated grill (broiler), on the barbecue or in a ridged pan, allowing about 6 minutes each side until cooked through. Test by piercing the thickest area of one chop with the tip of a knife, there should be no pink-tinged juices.

Transfer the pork to serving plates and top with spoonfuls of the butter.

teriyaki beef skewers with spring onion and cucumber salsa

This Japanese-inspired dish is just about as easy as it gets. You can even buy ready-made teriyaki sauce if you don't have the flavourings in your kitchen cupboard. Serve with sticky Asian or long grain rice.

Serves 4

60 ml (4 tablespoons) dark soy sauce

60 ml (4 tablespoons) mirin

55g (2 oz) light muscovado (brown) sugar

650 g (1 lb 7 oz) beef skirt (from the rump end) or rump steak

FOR THE SALSA

1 small cucumber

4 spring onions (scallions)

30 ml (2 tablespoons) rice wine vinegar

1 tablespoon caster (superfine) sugar

15 ml (1 tablespoon) groundnut or vegetable oil

To make the teriyaki sauce, put the soy sauce, mirin and sugar in a small saucepan and heat gently until the sugar dissolves. Bring to the boil and let the mixture bubble for a couple of minutes until slightly reduced and syrupy. Tip into a shallow dish.

Trim off any fat from the beef. Cut lengthways into 1 cm (½ in) thick slices. Cut the slices into strips each about 2 cm (¾ in) wide. Add the meat to the dish and turn the beef in the teriyaki sauce until coated. Leave to marinate for 10 minutes.

Thread the strips of beef onto 8 skewers, if necessary cutting the pieces of meat so they're fairly evenly distributed between the skewers.

To make the salsa, peel the cucumber and cut in half lengthways. Use a teaspoon to scrape out the seeds from the centre. Chop the cucumber flesh into small dice and put in a bowl. Trim and finely chop the spring onions and add to the bowl. Add the vinegar, sugar and oil and mix well. Turn into a small serving dish.

Cook the beef skewers under a preheated grill (broiler) or on the barbecue for 2–3 minutes, turning and basting with the excess marinade. Serve with the salsa.

merguez lamb burgers

Merguez is an intense mixture of spices used to flavour the most delicious Moroccan sausages. A similar combination of spices gives burgers a really appetizing twist. Buy good-quality lamb mince or better still, make your own (see page 30). Serve on burger buns with mayonnaise or, for a change, try them tucked into toasted pitta breads with shredded iceberg lettuce and a fruity chutney.

Serves 4

2 teaspoons cumin seeds

2 teaspoons coriander seeds

2 teaspoons fennel seeds

600 g (1 lb 5 oz) minced lamb

½ small red onion, finely chopped

½ teaspoon cayenne pepper

1 tablespoon ground paprika

2 garlic cloves, crushed

salt and freshly ground black pepper

a little vegetable oil, for brushing

Put all the seeds in a dry frying pan and heat for 2–3 minutes, shaking the pan frequently to lightly toast them. Tip into a pestle and mortar (or use a small bowl and the end of a rolling pin) and lightly crush.

Put the lamb mince in a bowl and add the onion, toasted seeds, cayenne pepper, paprika, garlic and a little salt and pepper. Mix well until the ingredients are thoroughly combined. This is much easier and quicker if you use your hands.

Divide the mixture into four equal-size portions and mould each into a ball. Flatten into burger shapes about 2 cm (¾ in) thick.

Prepare the barbecue or line a grill (broiler) tray with foil. Brush both sides of the burgers lightly with oil and cook for 4–5 minutes on each side until deep golden and cooked through.

steak with sweet chilli and butter bean salad

This recipe makes a relatively small amount of prime meat go a long way as it is mixed with butter beans to make a great main-meal barbecue salad. If you tend to cook meat right through, give this rare cooked steak a chance – it's so delicious with the spicy salad.

Serves 4

1 teaspoon hot smoked paprika

¼ teaspoon celery salt

350 g (12 oz) fillet steak in one piece, cut from
    the thin end

75 ml (5 tablespoons) groundnut or vegetable oil

2 x 400 g (14 oz) cans butter (lima) beans, rinsed
    and drained

2 shallots, thinly sliced

50 g (2 oz) rocket

60 ml (4 tablespoons) sweet chilli sauce

finely grated zest and juice of 1 lime

Mix together the paprika and celery salt and rub all over the surface of the meat. Brush 10 ml (2 teaspoons) of the oil over the meat and leave to stand for 15 minutes.

Tip the butter beans into a large bowl and stir in the shallots and rocket. Mix the remaining oil with 45 ml (3 tablespoons) of the sweet chilli sauce and the lime zest and juice.

Cook the beef on a preheated barbecue for about 10 minutes, turning frequently until crisp and browned on the outside but still pink in the centre. Alternatively, line a grill (broiler) rack with foil and grill (broil) the meat, turning it frequently for a similar time. Remove from the heat and brush with the remaining chilli sauce. Leave to stand for 5 minutes.

Toss the salad with the dressing. Thinly slice the beef and add to the salad. Mix together gently and serve.

chicken and halloumi kebabs

If you are mixing ingredients on skewers that take varying times to cook, it pays to part-cook the ingredients that take longest first so that everything cooks evenly. This applies particularly to chicken and pork, which should always be cooked through. In this recipe the chicken is gently poached first.

Makes 8

12 skinned and boned chicken thighs, quartered

500 ml (18 fl oz) chicken stock

several sprigs of oregano

10 g (¼ oz) mint

16 bay leaves

250 g (9 oz) halloumi cheese

FOR THE DRESSING

30 ml (2 tablespoons) lemon juice

60 ml (4 tablespoons) olive oil

1 garlic clove, crushed

1 teaspoon Dijon mustard

1 teaspoon caster (superfine) sugar

salt and freshly ground black pepper

Fit the chicken pieces snugly in a single layer in a frying pan. Add the stock, oregano and half the mint. Bring to a gentle simmer so the stock is just bubbling and cook for 10 minutes until the chicken is cooked through. Leave to cool in the stock.

Soak the bay leaves in hot water for 5 minutes to soften. Cut the halloumi into 1 cm (½ in) thick slices then cut the slices into chunks that are similar in diameter to the chicken. Thread the chicken, halloumi and bay leaves on 8 small skewers, bending the bay leaves in half if they are large before threading.

Mix together the lemon juice, olive oil, garlic, mustard, sugar, salt and pepper in a small bowl. Finely chop the remaining mint, discarding the stalks and add to the bowl.

Prepare the barbecue or line a grill (broiler) tray with foil. Cook the kebabs for about 5 minutes until the chicken begins to colour and the halloumi is soft and golden, turning frequently and basting with the mint dressing. Serve with the remaining dressing spooned over.

barbecued poussins with indian spices

These little chickens always seem to have more flavour than a standard chicken and they grill and barbecue well. You do, however, need to watch them closely and keep turning them to ensure even cooking. Serve with mango chutney and warmed naan breads that you can heat at the side of the fire, under a low grill (broiler) or in a ridged pan.

Serves 4

15 cardamom pods

1 teaspoon fennel seeds

2 teaspoons coriander seeds

2 teaspoons mustard seeds

½ teaspoon crushed dried chillies

2 cloves garlic, crushed

2 tablespoons vegetable oil

4 poussins, spatchcocked and skewered
   (see page 112)

salt

Crush the cardamom pods using a pestle and mortar or a small bowl and the end of a rolling pin. Pick out the shells and crush the seeds a little further. Add the fennel, coriander, mustard and dried chillies and pound until the seeds are crushed as finely as possible. A small spice or coffee grinder will do this job in seconds.

Mix together the garlic, oil and spices and rub the mixture all over both sides of each poussin. Place in a large shallow dish, cover loosely and chill for at least 1 hour or up to 8 hours.

Prepare the barbecue or line a grill (broiler) tray with foil. Cook the poussins, turning them frequently for about 25–30 minutes until cooked through. Test by piercing the thickest areas of the thighs and breast meat; the juices should run clear. Pull out the skewers, cut each poussin in half and serve sprinkled with a little salt.

spice-crusted belly pork

This recipe combines two cooking methods in one. First the pork is cooked slowly in the oven over a long time so that it is meltingly tender, then it is finished on the barbecue to colour, crisp and add extra flavour. The result is a fabulous tasting piece of meat that is great with simple salads and buttery apple sauce.

Serves 6

1 tablespoon fennel seeds, crushed

1½ teaspoons freshly ground black pepper

1 teaspoon salt

1 teaspoon ground allspice

finely grated zest of 2 lemons

3 garlic cloves, crushed

3 tablespoons light muscovado (brown) sugar

1.5 kg (3 lb 5 oz) belly pork, skinned

Preheat the oven to 150°C/300°F/Gas mark 2. Mix together the fennel seeds, pepper, salt, allspice, lemon zest, garlic and sugar. Rub the mixture over all the surfaces of the meat. Place in a roasting tin (pan), fat side uppermost, and cook for 3½–4 hours or until very tender.

Prepare the barbecue. Transfer the meat to the barbecue and cook for about 20 minutes, turning the meat until it's evenly browned on all sides. Alternatively, preheat the grill (broiler) to a moderately hot setting and brown the pork on all sides. Transfer to a serving plate and slice the meat into pieces.

Braising, Stewing and Casseroling

Braising, stewing and casseroling are similar cooking methods in that they are all slow and gentle and generally use tougher, cheaper cuts of meat immersed partially or fully in stock, wine, beer or other liquids. This form of cooking enables the fats and connective tissues within the meat to break down and tenderize the meat, while adding flavour to both the meat and the cooking juices. These are 'comfort dishes' that can be enjoyed from bowls with forks or spoons, using creamy mash, bread, couscous or dumplings to mop up the delicious juices.

There are some subtle differences between the three cooking methods. Braising usually refers to a single joint of meat or large pieces such as lamb shanks, semi-submerged in juices and cooked in the oven or on the stove top. Stewing uses smaller pieces of meat, almost entirely covered in liquid and likewise cooked on the stove top. Casseroles are similar to stews, but are generally cooked in a large pot in the oven. The meats are usually seared first to brown and caramelize the surface, then mixed with vegetables, herbs and other flavourings that mingle with the cooking juices to provide a delicious, flavour-packed sauce. Recipes entitled 'daube' or 'ragout' fall into these categories and are specific to one region or country's cuisine. Like all slow-cooked dishes, accurate cooking times are not essential so you can leave the dish to cook unattended, assured that you'll have a fabulous meal ready and waiting when you return.

Braising, stewing and casseroling tips

- Don't rush the browning stage as a well-seared surface on the meat will provide extra flavour and colour to your finished dish (see page 86).
- If cooking on the stove top, check frequently to see that the liquid isn't boiling too fiercely, otherwise the meat will be tough and the flavour impaired. The liquid should be barely bubbling. If you can't get the heat low enough, move the pan to one side of the heat.
- A little flour is often used to thicken wine- or stock-based liquids. And flour is used to coat the meat before browning or is added to fried vegetables before adding the liquid. If you don't use all the flour for coating meat, tip in the excess before adding liquids or you'll end up with thinner juices than you might like.
- If stewing meat prior to making a pie, allow yourself enough time to cook and cool the meat before assembling the pie. For convenience you might find it easier to cook the meat the day before.

Using a slow cooker

The braises, stews and casseroles in this chapter are great for cooking in electric free-standing slow cookers, using exactly the same methods and ingredients but transferring them to the slow cooker after preparing and frying. There's barely any liquid lost during slow-cooking so if making a stew or casserole covered in liquid you'll need to reduce the quantity by about a third. Meat dishes can be cooked effectively on the 'low' setting for about 8 hours.

Cooking ahead

Another advantage of this cooking method is that dishes can be cooked, cooled, chilled and reheated the following day, or frozen for a later date. Dishes flavoured with strongly aromatic ingredients such as ginger and spices can benefit from cooking ahead as the flavours integrate and develop. Cool these dishes completely, transfer to a dish or bowl (unless you've used a ceramic casserole dish) and chill. Reheat thoroughly, usually for about 30 minutes before serving. This is also great for particularly fatty dishes such as Oxtail Stew where a layer of solid whitish fat will have set on the surface. This can be lifted off before reheating.

braised lamb shanks with tomatoes and olives

Lamb shanks, the thin bony end of the leg, make absolutely delicious slow-cooked dishes where the meat falls meltingly off the bone. The tomatoes and wine absorb all the sweet juices from the meat, making a meal that's great for any occasion. Generally you can allow one shank per person but if you buy particularly small ones you'll need to allow two. Serve on a bed of creamy polenta.

Serves 4

4 lamb shanks, each weighing about 500 g (1 lb 2 oz)

salt and freshly ground black pepper

45 ml (3 tablespoons) olive oil

1 onion, chopped

4 garlic cloves, finely chopped

800 g (1 lb 12 oz) canned plum tomatoes

150 ml (5 fl oz) red wine

50 g (2 oz) can anchovy fillets, drained and chopped

2 tablespoons chopped oregano

1 tablespoon dark or light muscovado (molasses or brown) sugar

50 g (2 oz) pitted black olives

Preheat the oven to 160°C/325°F/Gas mark 3. Season the lamb shanks on all sides with salt and pepper. Heat 30 ml (2 tablespoons) of the oil in a flameproof casserole dish, add the lamb shanks two at a time and brown on all sides. Lift out onto a plate while you brown the remainder. Decant these to the plate.

Add the remaining oil and onion to the casserole and fry gently for 5 minutes, adding the garlic for the last minute. Add the tomatoes, wine, anchovies, oregano, sugar and a little salt and pepper. Bring the mixture to the boil and turn off the heat. Return the lamb shanks to the dish, pushing them down into the sauce. Cover with a lid, transfer to the oven and cook for 2 hours.

Stir the olives into the tomato sauce and return to the oven for another 1 hour or until the lamb is meltingly tender. Serve in shallow dishes, as it is, or on a bed of creamy polenta.

lamb with tahini, lemon and herbs

Look for jars of tahini among the specialist or ethnic ingredients on the supermarket shelves. It's a rich thick sesame paste that's great for Mediterranean, Middle Eastern and Indian cooking. Leftovers can be used up in hummous.

Serves 6

6 lamb chump chops (each weighing
  about 150 g/5½ oz)

1 teaspoon ground cumin

salt and freshly ground black pepper

30 ml (2 tablespoons) olive oil

4 courgettes (zucchini), sliced

1 fennel bulb, finely chopped

3 large sprigs rosemary

2 garlic cloves, crushed

450 ml (16 fl oz) lamb or chicken stock

2 tablespoons light muscovado (brown) sugar

finely grated zest and juice of 1 lemon

4 tablespoons finely chopped parsley

75 g (3 oz) tahini paste

Preheat the oven to 160°C/325°F/Gas mark 3. Rub the lamb chops with the cumin, salt and pepper.

Heat 15 ml (1 tablespoon) of the oil in a large frying pan and fry the lamb for several minutes on each side until deep golden. Transfer to a casserole dish.

Add the courgettes to the frying pan and fry gently for a couple of minutes on each side until lightly browned. Transfer to a plate.

Add the remaining oil and fennel to the frying pan and fry gently for 5 minutes. Add the rosemary, garlic, stock and sugar and bring just to the boil. Pour over the lamb and cover with a lid. Transfer to the oven and cook for 50 minutes or until the lamb is completely tender.

Stir in the lemon zest and juice, parsley and tahini paste. Scatter the courgettes on top and return to the oven for 10 minutes. Check the seasoning and serve with long-grain rice.

confit of guinea fowl

To confit meat is to preserve it by sealing it in fat. This technique is usually done with goose and duck but guinea fowl, which is richer and slightly gamier than chicken, is also really good. The meat is lightly salted to extract moisture and develop the flavour then cooked slowly and gently in duck or goose fat until completely tender. After cooling and sealing in the same fat it will keep for some time. Once it's heated through, and the surface skin crisped, the meat has a lovely rich flavour and is delicious with a fruit chutney, caramelized onions, lentils or chips (fries).

Serves 3–4

15 g (½ oz) salt

½ teaspoon freshly ground black pepper

1 tablespoon chopped thyme

3 garlic cloves, crushed

1 guinea fowl, jointed (see page 38)

400 g (14 oz) goose or duck fat

Mix together the salt, pepper, thyme and garlic. Rub all over the guinea fowl pieces and put in a shallow non-metallic dish. Cover loosely and chill for 24–48 hours.

Preheat the oven to 150°C/300°F/Gas mark 2. Scrape the garlic mixture off the pieces and reserve. Pat the guinea fowl pieces dry on kitchen paper. Melt 1 tablespoon of the fat in a large frying pan and fry the pieces (in batches if your pan isn't large enough) until golden. Drain to a casserole dish in which the pieces fit quite snugly. Tip in the reserved garlic mixture.

Tip the remaining fat into the frying pan and heat gently to melt. Pour carefully over the guinea fowl so the pieces are almost covered. Cover and cook in the oven for 1¼ hours then leave to cool in the fat.

Drain the pieces of guinea fowl to a large sterilized clip-top preserving jar or an earthenware dish. Cover with the fat and leave to solidify. Chill for up to 6 months.

To serve, preheat the oven to 200°C/400°F/Gas mark 6. Lift the meat from the fat, scraping off as much as possible and put in a roasting tin (pan). Cook for 15–20 minutes until heated right through before serving (keep the fat, which will last for a few more months, for delicious roast potatoes, see page 198).

braised beef with ginger beer and pumpkin

All the meat around the shoulder area of beef is fabulous for braising and stewing. You'll need to ask for the beef in one piece, as much of the meat from this part of the animal is sold sliced or diced.

Serves 6

1.25 kg (2 lb 12 oz) braising or chuck steak in one piece, rolled and tied

2 tablespoons plain (all-purpose) flour

salt and freshly ground black pepper

30 ml (2 tablespoons) vegetable oil

2 onions, chopped

3 carrots, sliced

3 bay leaves

1 cinnamon stick

1 medium-hot red chilli, deseeded and thinly sliced

60 ml (4 tablespoons) tomato purée

700 ml (1¼ pt) strong ginger beer

1 beef or vegetable stock cube, crumbled

600 g (1 lb 5 oz) pumpkin

Preheat the oven to 150°C/300°F/Gas mark 2. If the beef has not already been tied into a neat shape for cooking, tie lengths of string at 3 cm (1¼ in) intervals around it. Season the flour with salt and pepper and use to coat the meat.

Heat the oil in a flameproof casserole dish, add the meat and fry until browned on all sides, including the ends, turning it slowly in the oil. Lift out onto a plate. Add the onion and carrots to the casserole and fry gently for another 5 minutes. Tip in any excess flour left from coating the meat. Push the vegetables to the sides and return the meat to the centre of the dish. Add the bay leaves, cinnamon, chilli, tomato purée, ginger beer and stock cube. Bring just to the boil.

Cover with a lid and cook in the oven for 1½ hours. While the casserole is cooking, remove any seeds from the pumpkin, cut away the skin, then chop the flesh into small chunks. Add the pumpkin to the casserole and cook for another 45 minutes until the pumpkin is very tender. Season to taste and serve.

daube of beef
with tapenade

'Daube' is a French term for stew, in this case with a Mediterranean flavour. You can substitute stewing steak for braising steak though you might need to extend the cooking time slightly as it's a more economical cut. This dish is lovely with mashed potatoes, or seasonal vegetables and chunks of bread for mopping up the juices.

Serves 4–5

1 kg (2 lb 4 oz) braising steak, sliced

2 tablespoons plain (all-purpose) flour

salt and freshly ground black pepper

45 ml (3 tablespoons) olive oil

100 g (3½ oz) pancetta or streaky (fatty) bacon, chopped

2 onions, sliced

4 garlic cloves, crushed

several sprigs of thyme

300 ml (½ pint) red wine

300 ml (½ pint) beef stock

4 tablespoons sun-dried tomato purée

5 tablespoons tapenade

Preheat the oven to 150°C/300°F/Gas mark 2. Cut the braising steak into large chunks, each measuring about 5 cm (2 in) in diameter. Season the flour with salt and pepper and dust the meat in it. Heat 30 ml (2 tablespoons) of the oil in a flameproof casserole dish and fry the meat in batches until thoroughly browned, transferring each batch to a plate with a slotted spoon.

Once all the meat has been browned and drained, add the pancetta or bacon and onions to the pan and fry gently for 6–8 minutes until beginning to colour. Stir in any excess flour and cook for 1 minute. Return the meat to the casserole with the garlic, thyme, wine, stock and tomato purée. Bring to the boil and cover with a lid.

Cook in the oven for 2½ hours or until the meat is very tender. Stir in the tapenade and cook for another 15 minutes. Check the seasoning and serve.

guinness and oxtail casserole

Meat near the bone is said to have extra flavour, which is certainly true of oxtail. It also contains a lot of fat that is best skimmed off the surface before serving. The best way to do this is to make the casserole a day in advance, cool and allow it to set then lift away the fat from the surface before reheating thoroughly.

Serves 4

2 tablespoons plain (all-purpose) flour

1 tablespoon dry mustard

salt

2 kg (4 lb 8 oz) oxtail, cut into 4–5 cm
(1½–2 in) pieces

25 g (1 oz) butter

15 ml (1 tablespoon) vegetable oil

1 onion, chopped

1 leek, chopped

2 celery sticks, chopped

300 ml (½ pint) Guinness, or other dry stout

300 ml (½ pint) beef stock

2 tablespoons black treacle (molasses)

Preheat the oven to 160°C/325°F/Gas mark 3. Mix together the flour, mustard and salt and use to coat the pieces of oxtail. Melt the butter with the oil in a flameproof casserole and brown the oxtail, half at a time, until deep golden on all sides. Drain to a plate.

Add the onion, leek and celery to the casserole and fry gently, stirring frequently for about 10 minutes until softened and beginning to colour. Stir in any excess flour and cook for 1 minute. Add the Guinness, stock and treacle to the casserole and bring to a gentle simmer. Return the oxtail to the dish, pushing the pieces down into the liquid.

Cover with a lid and cook in the oven for about 1¾ hours or until the meat can be pulled easily from the bone. Check the seasoning and serve with root vegetables and mashed potatoes.

winter lamb stew
with dumplings

This is comfort food at its best and so easy to make. Lamb shoulder is sweet and tender and perfect for slow cooking. Buy a boned shoulder or, if you can only get a bone-in shoulder, buy that and bone it yourself. All you need is a sharp knife and a sturdy board. It's really very easy and is simply a matter of cutting away the meat from around the bones. Your cutting needn't be neat or uniform.

Serves 4

900 g (1 lb 10 oz) boned shoulder of lamb
salt and freshly ground black pepper
30 ml (2 tablespoons) vegetable oil
1 large onion, chopped
500 g (1 lb 2 oz) leeks, trimmed and chopped
3 bay leaves
1.4 litres (2½ pints) lamb or chicken stock
85 g (3 oz) pearl barley

FOR THE DUMPLINGS

150 g (5½ oz) self-raising (self-rising) flour
75 g (2½ oz) beef or vegetable suet (chilled, grated shortening)
2 tablespoons chopped mint
2 tablespoons chopped parsley
120 ml (4 fl oz) cold water

If the lamb is in one piece, cut it into 2.5 cm (1in) chunks, discarding any large areas of fat. Season with salt and pepper.

Heat 15 ml (1 tablespoon) of the oil in a large frying pan and fry the lamb in batches until browned, transferring each batch to a large saucepan or flameproof casserole using a slotted spoon. Once all the lamb has been browned, add the remaining oil to the pan with the onion and leeks, and fry gently for 5 minutes. Tip out over the meat.

Add the bay leaves and stock to the frying pan and bring just to the boil. Pour over the lamb and vegetables and stir in the pearl barley. Cover with a lid and cook the stew on the lowest heat for about $1\frac{1}{2}$ hours until the lamb and pearl barley are tender and the juices have thickened.

To make the dumplings while the lamb is cooking, 30 minutes before you are ready to sit down and eat: put the flour, suet, mint and parsley in a bowl with a little salt and pepper. Stir in the cold water and mix to a soft dough. If the mixture feels a bit dry and crumbly add a dash more water but don't make it too sticky.

Once the lamb is tender, season the stew to taste. Using a dessertspoon place spoonfuls of the dumpling mixture on the surface, spacing them slightly apart. Cover with the lid and cook the stew gently for another 15–20 minutes until the dumplings have risen and have a 'fluffy' texture. Serve in shallow bowls.

lamb, date and pistachio tagine

Tagines are rich fragrant dishes that form the core of traditional Moroccan cooking. They can be described as braises or stews and are conventionally cooked in the oven in a conical lidded earthenware pot – though a casserole dish works equally well. Serve with a steaming pot of light and fluffy couscous (see page 202).

Serves 4

800 g (1 lb 12 oz) boned shoulder of lamb

60 ml (4 tablespoons) olive oil

1 cinnamon stick, halved

1 teaspoon ground cumin

2 onions, sliced

25 g (1 oz) fresh root ginger, grated

2 garlic cloves, thinly sliced

1 teaspoon saffron strands

150 g (5½ oz) pitted dates, roughly chopped

45 ml (3 tablespoons) clear honey

30 ml (2 tablespoons) lemon juice

salt

50 g (2 oz) shelled pistachio nuts

chopped fresh coriander (cilantro), to garnish

Preheat the oven to 160°C/325°F/Gas mark 3. Cut the lamb into large chunks about 4 cm (1½ in) in diameter. Heat half the olive oil in a flameproof casserole and add the cinnamon and cumin. Add the lamb and turn it in the spicy oil until coated. Continue to fry the meat gently, turning it until lightly browned, 3–4 minutes. Drain the meat to a plate with a slotted spoon.

Heat the remaining oil in the casserole. Add the onions and fry gently for 5 minutes, adding the ginger and garlic for the last couple of minutes. Return the meat to the dish and crumble in the saffron strands. Add 400 ml (14 fl oz) cold water and bring to a gentle simmer.

Cover with a lid and cook in the oven for 1½ hours or until the lamb is very tender. Stir in the dates, honey, lemon juice and a little salt, if necessary. Return to the oven for 10 minutes.

Put the pistachio nuts in a heatproof bowl, cover with boiling water and leave for 1 minute. Drain and place the nuts between several sheets of kitchen paper. Rub the paper against the nuts to remove as much of the brown skin as you can. Chop the nuts and scatter over the tagine with the coriander to garnish.

chicken and red onion stifado

A 'stifado' is a slow-cooked meat stew, usually flavoured with onions, garlic and wine. The chicken is buried under a mass of fried onions that keeps it really moist and succulent, and the red wine and vinegar sauce is reduced down so the flavour is intense and delicious.

Serves 4

½ teaspoon ground allspice

salt and freshly ground black pepper

1.25–1.5 kg (2 lb 12 oz–3 lb 5 oz) chicken, jointed

45 ml (3 tablespoons) olive oil

4 large red onions, sliced

1 tablespoon light muscovado (brown) sugar

3 garlic cloves, crushed

300 ml (10 fl oz) red wine

60 ml (4 tablespoons) red wine vinegar

3 tablespoons sun-dried tomato purée

2 tablespoons chopped oregano, plus extra
   to garnish

Preheat the oven to 160°C/325°F/Gas mark 3. Sprinkle the ground allspice over the surface of the chicken pieces. Season well with salt and pepper and rub into the skin with your fingers.

Heat 30 ml (2 tablespoons) of the oil in a large flameproof casserole and fry the chicken pieces in batches until browned on all sides. Lift the pieces out onto a plate as you go.

Once all the chicken pieces are browned add the remaining oil, onion and sugar to the pan and fry over a low heat for about 15 minutes, stirring frequently, until deep golden. Stir in the garlic and fry for another couple of minutes.

Add the wine and vinegar to the pan and bring to the boil. Cook quickly until the liquid has reduced by about a third. Stir in the tomato purée and chopped oregano. Return the chicken pieces to the dish, nestling them down into the onions. Cover with a lid and cook in the oven for about 1½ hours or until the chicken is cooked through and the juices are thick. Scatter with oregano leaves and serve.

Baking

Baked dishes are a feast of flavours contained in one delicious pot, bubbling and crispy-crusted on the outside and packed with flavour and tenderness inside. Baking covers a wide range of meats, recipe styles, flavours and textures as well as cooking techniques covered in the other chapters. The meats can be prime or cheap cuts, part-cooked first on the hob or cooked entirely in the oven. What all the recipes share is that the meat has some sort of covering – pastry, a thick layer of vegetables, breadcrumbs, foil or a lid – to stop the heat from drying out the dish. These recipes are great for preparing ahead, ready for finishing in the oven just before you plan to eat.

Baking tips

- The usual rules for browning meat apply to baked recipes. The meat won't brown any more once it is submerged under other ingredients.
- Allow enough time to cook and cool the filling for a pastry-lidded pie. If you try and cover a hot pie filling with chilled pastry, it'll melt onto the meat and the texture and appearance of the pastry will be spoilt.
- Shallow pie dishes in two or three sizes (for single serving, two or three portions and larger gatherings) are worth having in the kitchen cupboard. That way you can split the quantities in a recipe between dishes that are more practical for your particular needs. If buying new dishes, choose ones you love and want to take to the table.
- Crusty topped pies and other baked dishes look fabulous when they're served hot from the oven, bubbling around the edges and golden crusted. Have a large sturdy board ready on the table to protect it and catch any spillages.
- Potato and pastry-topped pies freeze well. Cook and cool the filling, add the potato or pastry lid and freeze before baking. Transfer to the fridge the day before cooking and bake as in the recipe so the pie looks golden crusted and freshly cooked.
- Baked dishes make good 'one pot' food where root vegetables, pasta or pastry is included. You might simply want a seasonal green vegetable or mixed salad to accompany.
- It goes without saying that dishes come piping hot out of the oven. To enjoy their full flavour it's best to let them stand for 15 minutes or so before serving. Dishes like lasagne will also thicken slightly making them easier to serve.

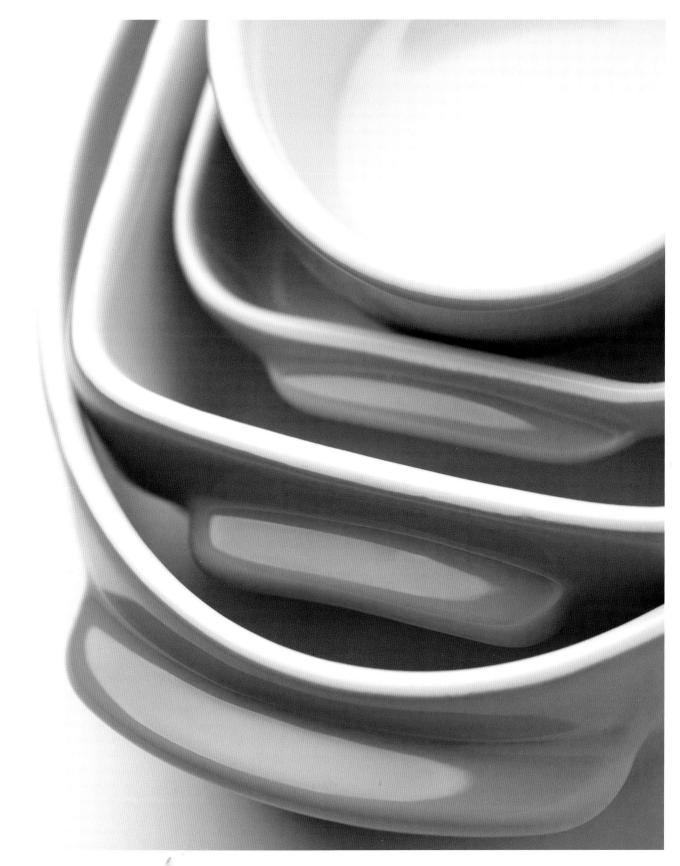

cottage pie with parsnip mash

*This recipe is richer than a basic cottage pie, with herbs, garlic and Worcestershire sauce giving extra flavour.
Some of us love baked beans in our pie, others don't, so include or leave out as you like.*

Serves 4

50 g (2 oz) butter

30 ml (2 tablespoons) vegetable oil

500 g (1 lb 2 oz) lean minced beef

1 onion, chopped

3 carrots, chopped

2 celery sticks, chopped

2 garlic cloves, crushed

1 tablespoon plain (all-purpose) flour

300 ml (10 fl oz) beef or chicken stock

45 ml (3 tablespoons) Worcestershire sauce

30 ml (2 tablespoons) tomato paste

salt and freshly ground black pepper

400 g (14 oz) can baked beans

500 g (1 lb 2 oz) floury potatoes

500 g (1 lb 2 oz) parsnips

60 ml (4 tablespoons) milk

50 g (2 oz) Parmesan or mature Cheddar
    cheese, grated

Melt half the butter with the oil in a large saucepan. Add the minced beef and fry for
6–8 minutes until browned, stirring and breaking up the meat with the edge of the spoon.

Add the onion, carrots, celery and garlic and cook for another 5 minutes, stirring frequently.
Add the flour and cook for another minute. Pour in the stock, stirring to mix, then add the
Worcestershire sauce, tomato paste and a little seasoning. Cover and cook gently for
30 minutes until the sauce has thickened and the meat is tender. Stir in the baked beans
and tip into a shallow ovenproof dish.

Preheat the oven to 190°C/375°F/Gas mark 5. Cut the potatoes and parsnips into similarly
sized chunks and put in a saucepan. Cover with cold water, add a little salt and bring to the
boil. Reduce the heat and simmer for about 15 minutes or until tender. Drain and return to the
saucepan. Add the remaining butter, the milk, all but 4 tablespoons of the cheese and a little
black pepper. Mash well.

Spoon the mash onto the meat sauce and spread it out in an even layer. Use a fork to break
up the surface so you'll get a good, crispy crust. Scatter with the cheese and bake for about
40 minutes until golden.

pork cheek, mushroom and perry pie

Most meat pies are cooked in two stages. Firstly the meat is casseroled, as in this recipe, then topped with pastry and baked. You may need to order pork cheeks from the butcher. They're not too readily available, but like ox cheek, make an economical treat of a meal. Make the filling a day in advance so it's cooled and ready for its pastry lid.

Serves 6

1 kg (2 lb 2 oz) pork cheeks

3 tablespoons plain (all-purpose) flour, plus extra
　　for dusting

salt and freshly ground black pepper

50 g (2 oz) butter

30 ml (2 tablespoons) vegetable oil

250 g (9 oz) chestnut mushrooms, sliced

2 onions, chopped

500 ml (18 fl oz) perry or cider

150 ml (5 fl oz) pork or chicken stock

2 tablespoons chopped sage

45 ml (3 tablespoons) crème fraîche

375 g (13 oz) puff pastry or Butter Shortcrust
　　Pastry (see page 204)

beaten egg, to glaze

sea salt

Preheat the oven to 150°C/300°F/Gas mark 2. Cut the pork cheeks into 2 cm (¾ in) cubes. Season the flour with salt and pepper and use to coat the pork. Heat half the butter and oil in a flameproof casserole and fry the pork in batches until browned, draining each batch to a plate with a slotted spoon.

Add half the remaining butter to the casserole and fry the mushrooms quickly to lightly colour. Drain to a separate plate. Heat the remaining butter and oil and fry the onions for about 5 minutes until softened, adding any leftover flour for the last minute. Gradually stir in the perry and stock. Return the meat to the casserole with the sage. Bring to the boil, cover with a lid and cook in the oven for 2½ hours or until the pork is very tender. Stir in the mushrooms and crème fraîche, check the seasoning and leave to cool completely.

Turn into a pie dish with a capacity of about 1.2 litres (2 pints). The liquid level should be about 2 cm (¾ in) from the rim of the dish. If there's too much, pour it into a small saucepan for reheating later and serving separately in a small gravy boat.

Raise the oven temperature to 190°C/375°F/Gas mark 5. Roll out the pastry on a lightly floured surface until slightly larger than the top of the dish. Brush the rim with water and place the pastry, trimming off the excess around the edges. Press a floured fork around the rim to decorate and make a hole in the centre to allow the steam to escape. You can, if you like, use the trimmings to decorate the pie. Brush with beaten egg and sprinkle with sea salt. Bake for about 45 minutes until deep golden.

rabbit hotpot with juniper and crème fraîche

A farmed rabbit is larger, meatier and milder in flavour than a wild rabbit so it's a good introduction to this delicious game if you've not eaten it before. Ask the butcher to portion it for you.

1 tablespoon plain (all-purpose) flour

salt and freshly ground black pepper

1 kg (2 lb 4 oz) rabbit, jointed

10 juniper berries

50 g (2 oz) butter

1 tablespoon vegetable oil

2 onions, sliced

2 garlic cloves, crushed

1 tablespoon chopped thyme

1 kg (2 lb 4 oz) large potatoes, thinly sliced

300 ml (10 fl oz) chicken or game stock

60 ml (4 tablespoons) crème fraîche

Preheat the oven to 160°C/325°F/Gas mark 3. Season the flour with salt and pepper, and use to coat the pieces of rabbit. Crush the juniper berries using a pestle and mortar.

Melt half the butter with the oil in a frying pan and fry the rabbit portions in batches until golden on all sides, decanting the pieces to a shallow ovenproof dish once browned. Add the onions to the frying pan and fry gently for 6–8 minutes or until pale golden, adding the garlic, thyme and juniper for the last couple of minutes. Tip out over the rabbit. Layer up the potatoes in overlapping slices on top of the rabbit.

Add the chicken or game stock and crème fraîche to the frying pan and bring to the boil. Season with a little salt and pepper and pour over the potatoes. Cover with a lid or foil and cook in the oven for 1 hour. Melt the remaining butter and brush over the surface of the potatoes. Raise the oven temperature to 190°C/375°F/Gas mark 5 and bake for another 20–30 minutes to lightly brown the surface of the potatoes.

honey and ginger-glazed ribs

Finger-licking dishes don't come stickier than this! Choose meaty pork ribs to make them worth the effort of frequent basting to build up the delicious glaze.

Serves 4

1.25 kg (2 lb 12 oz) pork spare ribs

50 g (2 oz) fresh root ginger

2 garlic cloves, crushed

4 tablespoons clear honey

finely grated zest and juice of 2 limes

30 ml (2 tablespoons) white wine vinegar

3 tablespoons tomato purée

30 ml (2 tablespoons) soy sauce

Arrange the ribs in a single layer in a shallow non-metallic dish.

Peel and grate the ginger into a bowl. Add the garlic, honey, lime zest and juice, vinegar, tomato purée and soy sauce. Pour the mixture over the ribs. Cover and chill for several hours or overnight.

Preheat the oven to 180°C/350°F/Gas mark 4. Lift the ribs out into a roasting tin (pan) and pour over the juices left in the dish. Bake for 45 minutes. Baste the ribs with the glaze and return to the oven for another 45 minutes or until the meat is tender. Baste the ribs several times as the glaze thickens so it coats them thickly.

cassoulet

Cassoulet is good to serve at any time of year. Use really well-flavoured garlicky sausages so that they flavour the other ingredients. Don't forget to soak the beans the day before you plan to make it.

Serves 6

500 g (1 lb 2 oz) dried haricot beans

750 g (1 lb 10 oz) skinned belly pork, cut in 2 cm (¾ in) cubes

60 ml (4 tablespoons) olive oil, goose or duck fat

3 duck legs, halved

12 garlic sausages, such as Toulouse

2 onions, roughly chopped

6 garlic cloves, skinned and left whole

4 bay leaves

1.2 litres (2 pints) chicken stock

salt and freshly ground black pepper

2 tablespoons tomato purée

½ teaspoon cloves

100 g (3½ oz) breadcrumbs

Put the beans in a bowl and cover with plenty of cold water. Leave to soak overnight. The next day drain the beans and put in a large saucepan. Cover with cold water and bring to the boil. Boil rapidly for 10 minutes then reduce the heat to a gentle simmer and cook for 30 minutes or until the beans are just beginning to soften. You should be able to crush one with a fork. Drain.

Heat the oil or fat in a frying pan and fry the pieces of pork until browned. Lift out onto a plate. Brown the sausages in the frying pan, then brown the duck legs. Drain to the plate.

Tip a third of the beans into a casserole. Put half the sausages, pork and duck pieces on top and scatter with half the onions, garlic and bay leaves. Add half the remaining beans, then the remaining meat, onion, garlic and bay leaves. Top with the remaining beans and season.

Preheat the oven to 150°C/300°F/Gas mark 2. Blend the stock in the frying pan with the tomato purée and cloves. Pour over the beans. The stock should just about cover the beans; if it doesn't, top up with a little hot water. Cover with a lid and bake for about 2 hours or until the beans are completely tender.

Sprinkle the breadcrumbs over the cassoulet and return to the oven, uncovered, for about 30 minutes or until the breadcrumbs are golden.

lasagne

This recipe gives you two dishes in one. A classic lasagne is made using a beef 'ragu' which is the exactly the same sauce used for bolognese, so stop at the end of the second step if you want to make a simple spaghetti bolognese. If you are short of time when making the lasagne, use a ready-made good-quality cheese sauce, but definitely make the meat sauce from scratch.

Serves 4

25 g (1 oz) butter

30 ml (2 tablespoons) olive oil

1 onion, finely chopped

1 celery stick, chopped

500 g (1 lb 2 oz) beef mince

200 ml (7 fl oz) dry white wine

60 ml (4 tablespoons) double (heavy) cream

3 tablespoons sun-dried tomato purée

400 g (14 oz) can chopped tomatoes

1 teaspoon caster (superfine) sugar

200 g (7 oz) lasagne pasta sheets

FOR THE CHEESE SAUCE

50 g (2 oz) butter

40 g (1½ oz) plain (all-purpse) flour

450 ml (16 fl oz) milk

85 g (3 oz) Parmesan cheese, grated

Melt 25 g (1 oz) of butter in a large saucepan with the oil. Add the onion and celery and cook gently for 5 minutes to soften. Add the beef and mix with the vegetables, breaking it up with the edge of the spoon. As soon as the beef has lost its redness, add the wine to the pan. Bring to the boil and boil until the wine has evaporated.

Stir in the cream, tomato purée, tomatoes and sugar and bring to the boil. Reduce the heat to its lowest setting, cover with a lid and cook gently for about 1 hour, stirring frequently until the sauce is thick, pulpy and tender. Leave to cool.

To make the cheese sauce, melt the butter in a small saucepan. Add the flour and cook over a gentle heat, stirring with a wooden spoon to make a paste. Remove from the heat and gradually blend in the milk, whisking well to avoid the sauce turning lumpy. Once all the milk has been added, return the pan to the heat and cook gently, stirring until thickened (use a whisk to beat out any lumps at this stage). Stir in all but 3 tablespoons of the cheese and season to taste with salt and pepper.

Preheat the oven to 180°C/350°F/Gas mark 4. Spoon a very thin layer of meat sauce into a shallow ovenproof dish. Drizzle with a few spoonfuls of the cheese sauce. Arrange some lasagne sheets on top, if necessary cutting them to fit in a single layer. Continue layering up the ingredients until the meat sauce and pasta have been used up. You should still have plenty of cheese sauce left. Spoon this on top and spread to the edges. Scatter with the reserved cheese and bake for about 45–50 minutes until the surface is golden and bubbling. Leave to stand for 10 minutes before serving.

pork and fennel picnic pie

This is really no more than a giant sausage roll but it shows just how simple this kind of dish is to prepare. Make and wrap the filling in pastry, pop it in the oven and take it still warm on a summer picnic, or serve simply for an easy supper. The pastry might split during baking, but that adds to its simple charm.
Serves 6

15 ml (1 tablespoon) vegetable oil

1 small onion, chopped

1 bulb fennel, chopped

450 g (1 lb) good-quality sausagemeat

250 g (9 oz) minced (ground) pork

2 teaspoons garam masala

salt and freshly ground black pepper

375 g (13 oz) puff pastry

flour, for dusting

beaten egg, to glaze

Preheat the oven to 220°C/425°F/Gas mark 7. Grease a large baking sheet. Heat the oil in a frying pan and gently fry the onion and fennel for 5 minutes to soften. Leave to cool.

Mix together the sausagemeat, minced pork, garam masala, onion, fennel and a little salt and pepper in a bowl – use your hands – it's much easier.

Dust the work surface with flour. Roll out the pastry to a 35 x 25 cm (14 x 10 in) rectangle. Turn the meat mixture out onto the surface and shape into a 33 cm (13 in) long sausage. Lift onto the pastry and roll up quite loosely in the pastry (if too tightly wrapped the pastry is more likely to split down its length during baking). Transfer to the baking sheet with the join underneath and pinch the ends together.

Brush the pastry with beaten egg. Make diagonal cuts 2 cm (¾ in) apart down the length of the pastry with a sharp knife. Bake for 20 minutes, then reduce the temperature to 180°C/250°F/Gas mark 4 and bake for another 25 minutes. Leave to cool for at least 15 minutes before slicing.

Poaching

Poaching is cooking meat by submerging it in liquid and cooking it either on the stove top or in the oven. Poaching means the meat is gently cooked in liquid that is barely shuddering. This method produces tender meat that is easy to slice and full of flavour. Usually meats are brought to the boil to get the cooking started and then reduced to the gentle poaching temperature so it cooks through very slowly.

This form of cooking is generally used for ham, bacon and poultry, and occasionally red meats, the most well-known of which is salt beef. The main purpose is to keep the meat moist and succulent and permeate it with flavour by adding vegetables, spices and herbs to the liquid which is usually stock, wine, beer or water. Poaching is not used as much as other forms of meat cooking but is worth adding to your repertoire. A homemade Glazed Ham, the type you might serve at Christmas, is a typical recipe using this cooking method so it's useful to know about it, even if you only try it once a year. After long and gentle poaching in seasoned liquid, the ham is spread with a sweet glaze and finished in the oven to give it a lovely caramelly crust.

The recipe on page 180 has a spicy orange flavour but you can experiment with other ingredients for a home-baked ham that's great served any time of year. Simply by poaching the ham in beer or cider with a few onions and celery sticks you'll produce a ham with a completely different and delicious flavour. The glaze can be any ingredient that sweetly contrasts with the saltiness of the ham. Try brown sugar, maple syrup, honey or treacle.

Poaching tips

- A large heavy saucepan will accommodate most joints of ham or a whole large chicken. A preserving pan is the next best thing, and is ideal for a large festive ham.
- The joint should fit reasonable snugly into the pan. This is particularly important if you're cooking the meat in wine, beer or stock as too much space around the meat will mean you'll have to use excessive amounts of costly ingredients. You will, however, need enough space to tuck in flavouring ingredients like onions, celery and carrots.
- Ideally, the meat should be totally submerged under the liquid. If the pan is too shallow for the joint and part of it is uncovered you can turn the meat occasionally

so all areas are submerged for most of the time. It also helps to use a lid as the steam created will help to keep any exposed areas moist. If you don't have a lid for the pan use foil tucked under the rim, or a baking sheet.

• Bear in mind that using a lid will also raise the temperature because the heat is trapped. Check frequently to make sure the liquid isn't bubbling away too fiercely. If the heat setting is at its lowest and the liquid is still bubbling, pull the pan to one side of the ring.

• After cooking, leave the meat to cool in the liquid unless the recipe states otherwise. This helps to keep it moist and juicy.

• Don't automatically discard the cooking liquid. If it's not used in the recipe (and doesn't taste too salty), keep it as a ready-made stock for favouring soups and stews. You might want to boil the liquid down to make it more concentrated and more convenient to store in the refrigerator or freezer.

• If poaching a boned piece of meat, add the bones to the liquid to add more flavour.

Soaking salty cuts

Bacon and gammon joints require soaking before cooking to remove the salt required to cure it. Do this the day before you want to cook the joint. Place the meat in a large bowl, preferably one in which the whole joint can be submerged. Cover with cold water and leave to stand in a cool place. On a warm day, change the water several times, covering the meat with cold water. A preserving pan is also useful for soaking a large piece of gammon.

Green or smoked?

Bacon and gammon cuts can be bought 'green' or 'smoked'. Smoked bacon has been cured and then smoked to give extra flavour. Green bacon is the traditional term for unsmoked bacon. It's a matter of personal choice as to which you buy. Both are cooked in the same way.

ham hock with creamy parsley sauce

Ham hocks make a bargain cut as they are removed from the fore and hindquarter leg cuts but still contain plenty of sweet, juicy meat. Long, slow cooking is essential to tenderize all the muscles and sinewy parts. If this is done well the meat can be pulled easily from the bone, and is great for serving with an old-fashioned parsley sauce. Alternatively, you can use the meat and stock in Pea and Ham Soup or simply cook a hock and have it ready in the refrigerator for shredding pieces off into sandwiches or salads.

Serves 4–5

2 ham hocks, each weighing about 1 kg (2 lb 4 oz)

2 onions, peeled and halved

4 celery sticks, quartered

4 carrots, quartered

4 bay leaves

1 tablespoon black peppercorns

FOR THE PARSLEY SAUCE

25 g (1 oz) butter

20 g (¾ oz) plain (all-purpose) flour

300 ml (½ pint) milk

15 g (½ oz) parsley, finely chopped

45 ml (3 tablespoons) single (light) cream

Soak the ham hocks in cold water for 24 hours.

Lift the ham from the water and place in a large saucepan. Cover with cold water and bring to the boil. Once the water is boiling, remove from the heat and drain off the water. Tuck the onions, celery, carrots and bay leaves around the ham and cover with more cold water. Add the peppercorns.

Bring the water once again to the boil then reduce the heat to its lowest setting. The water should be barely moving. Leave to cook very gently for 2½–3 hours or until the meat is very tender and a piece can be pulled easily from the joint. Turn off the heat and leave in the stock while making the sauce.

Melt the butter in a saucepan. Add the flour and cook stirring for 1 minute. Remove from the heat and gradually blend in the milk. Use a whisk if necessary to eliminate any lumps. Measure 300 ml (½ pint) of the ham stock into a jug and gradually blend this into the sauce. Stir in the parsley and cream. Return to the heat and cook gently, stirring with a wooden spoon until the sauce is smooth and thickened enough to coat the back of the spoon.

Lift the ham hocks from the stock and cut away the skin. Pull pieces of meat away from the bone and place on serving plates. Pour over the sauce.

chicken, herb and lemon pie

This is a fail-proof way of making a fabulous chicken pie. A whole chicken is poached in stock first so all the delicious goodness in the bones flavours the stock, which is then used to make the sauce. Poach the chicken up to a day in advance so it can cool in the liquid, staying juicy and moist.

Serves 5

1 chicken, about 1.5 kg (3 lb 5 oz)

1 onion, peeled and halved

1 lemon, sliced

3 bay leaves

300 g (10½ oz) shallots

25 g (1 oz) butter

3 tablespoons plain (all-purpose) flour

15 g (½ oz) chopped mixed herbs, thyme, parsley,
    tarragon, chervil

60 ml (4 tablespoons) crème fraîche

2 tablespoons capers, rinsed and drained

salt and freshly ground black pepper

Butter Shortcrust Pastry (see page 204)

flour, for dusting

beaten egg, to glaze

Rinse out the chicken and remove any trussing. Place in a saucepan in which it fits quite snugly. Add the onion, lemon and bay leaves to the pan and cover with cold water. Bring to the boil then reduce the heat to its lowest setting, cover and cook for about 1 hour, until the chicken is cooked through. Test by pushing a knife down through the chicken, it should go through easily. Leave the chicken to cool in the liquid.

Put the unpeeled shallots in a saucepan, cover with hot water and bring to the boil. Cook for 2 minutes then drain through a colander and rinse under cold running water. Peel away the skins leaving the shallots whole.

Lift the chicken from the stock and measure 600 ml (1 pint) of the stock into a jug (bowl). Melt the butter in a saucepan and tip in the flour. Cook, stirring for 1 minute. Remove from the heat and gradually blend in the stock using a whisk, if necessary, to remove any lumps. Return to the heat and cook gently, stirring with a wooden spoon until the sauce is slightly thickened. Stir in the herbs, crème fraîche, capers and seasoning to taste. Leave to cool.

Pull the chicken legs away from the carcass and use your fingers to remove all the leg meat, discarding the skin and bones. Pull away the breast meat, discard the skin. Remove all the remaining chicken meat from the carcass including the small amount of meat inside the wings. Chop all the meat into small pieces and place in a 1.75 litre (3 pint) pie dish with the shallots. Pour the sauce over the meat until it is no less than 1 cm (½ in) from the rim of the dish (any excess can be heated through and served separately).

Preheat the oven to 190°C/375°F/Gas 5. Roll out the pastry on a lightly floured surface until slightly larger than the top of the dish. Brush the rim with water and position the pastry, trimming off the excess around the edges. Crimp the edges with your fingers to decorate (or leave plain) and make a hole in the centre to allow the steam to escape. You can use the trimmings, if you like, to decorate the pie. Brush with beaten egg and bake for about 45 minutes until deep golden.

cardamom and seville orange glazed ham

If you cook a piece of ham this big you'll be rewarded with a substantial joint that will keep in the fridge for up to a week, providing the basis for delicious snacks and sandwiches. For a main meal, serve with a fruity coleslaw and potato salad.

Serves 6

2.5 kg (5 lb 8 oz) boned gammon joint

1.4 litres (2½ pints) fresh orange juice

2 small leeks, trimmed and roughly sliced

2 cinnamon sticks

1 tablespoon whole cloves

several bay leaves

6 tablespoons Seville (Temple) orange marmalade

1½ tablespoons cardamom pods, crushed and shells removed

2 teaspoons Dijon mustard

Soak the gammon in cold water for 24 hours, then transfer it to a large saucepan. Cover with cold water and bring to the boil. Remove from the heat and drain off the water. Add the leeks, cinnamon, cloves and bay leaves to the pan and pour in the orange juice. Top up with cold water until the gammon is covered.

Bring to the boil, then reduce the heat to its lowest setting. The water should be barely moving. Leave to cook very gently for 2 hours, checking the liquid level occasionally and topping up with water, if necessary. Leave to cool in the liquid.

Preheat the oven to 220°C/425°F/Gas mark 7. Lift the meat onto a board. Slice the skin away from the fat, checking to make sure you're not removing the fat. Use the tip of the knife to score deep cuts into the fat about 2 cm (¾ in) apart. Make more cuts in the opposite direction. Transfer the joint to a kitchen foil-lined roasting tin (pan) with the fat side uppermost.

Press the marmalade through a sieve into a bowl and stir in the crushed seeds and mustard. Brush the mixture over the gammon fat. Bake for about 20 minutes, basting frequently with the juices in the tin, until the glaze is golden. Serve warm or cold.

pork poached in milk

This recipe might sound a little odd but it's totally delicious. The pork cooks slowly and gently in the milk and takes on a sweet, creamy flavour and meltingly tender texture. To get the best from the garlic, scoop the tender flesh from the skin and return it to the sauce, or beat it into accompanying mash. Serve with creamy mashed potato and wilted spinach.

Serves 5–6

1.25 kg (2 lb 12 oz) pork loin, skinned,
    boned and rolled
salt and freshly ground black pepper
30 ml (2 tablespoons) olive oil

1 garlic head
1 large fennel
1.4 litres (2½ pints) milk

Season the pork on all sides with salt and pepper. Heat the oil in a frying pan and brown the pork thoroughly on all sides.

Transfer the pork to a saucepan or flameproof casserole dish in which it fits quite snugly. Cut the garlic head in half and add to the saucepan or casserole with the fennel. Pour in the milk. Bring the milk slowly to the boil, watching carefully to check that it doesn't boil over. Reduce the heat to its lowest setting and partially cover with a lid.

Cook gently for about 2 hours, turning the meat a couple of times so it cooks evenly. Test by piercing the meat with a knife – it should feel very tender. Once cooked, the milk will have mostly evaporated and turned golden.

Remove the meat to a carving platter or board and let stand for 15 minutes before serving. Strain the cooking liquid through a kitchen paper-lined sieve (strainer) and spoon the juices over the pork.

chicken, pepper and coconut soup

This is a soup for a main meal – rich and spicy and topped with delicious little cornmeal dumplings. Poaching the chicken legs first makes a simple well-flavoured stock, and the rest is really easy.

Serves 4

30 ml (2 tablespoons) vegetable oil

2 red (bell) peppers, deseeded and cut
  into small chunks

4 chicken legs, each cut in half through the joint

1 onion, chopped

1 tablespoon Cajun spice blend

3 garlic cloves, thinly sliced

1 red chilli, deseeded and finely chopped

400 ml (14 fl oz) can coconut cream

200 g (7 oz) can tomatoes

salt

FOR THE DUMPLINGS

100 g (3½ oz) self-raising (self-rising) flour

100 g (3½ oz) cornmeal

75 g (2½ oz) Gruyère cheese, grated

1 egg, beaten

45 ml (3 tablespoons) vegetable oil

85ml (3 fl oz) milk

Heat the oil in a pan. Add the peppers and fry gently for about 10 minutes. Transfer to a plate.

Add the chicken to the pan with the onion, spice blend, garlic and chilli. Pour over just enough cold water to cover the chicken – about 500 ml (18 fl oz). Bring to the boil and reduce the heat to its lowest setting. Cover and cook gently for 40 minutes, or until cooked through. Leave to cool for 30 minutes then remove from the pan.

For the dumplings, put the flour, cornmeal and cheese in a bowl and mix together. Add the egg and oil and enough milk using a round-bladed knife to mix the ingredients to a thick paste.

Once the chicken is cool enough to handle, pull the meat from the bone, shredding it and add to the pan with the coconut, tomatoes and peppers. Heat until the liquid is just bubbling. Take dessertspoonfuls of the cornmeal mixture and place on the surface of the soup. Cover, cook gently for 20 minutes or until the dumplings have risen slightly and are cooked through.

Basic Recipes

chicken stock

Good stock is a core part of good meat cooking and so much easier to make than you might think. Never throw away bones, you've paid for them and should reap every bit of value from them. If you don't have sufficient bones from the joint you've bought, save them up in the freezer, clearly labelled, until you have a worthwhile amount. Butchers will also sell bones cheaply as not everyone can be bothered with them A great stock can be made using the leftover carcass from a roast chicken or by collecting up chicken bones in the freezer from various chicken meals. If you get giblets with the chicken, add these too, plus any scrapings from the carving board.

Makes about 1 litre (1¾ pints)

1 large chicken carcass, plus leg and wing bones, trimmings and giblets	several bay leaves
1 onion, unpeeled and quartered	several sprigs of thyme
1 leek, roughly chopped	2 teaspoons black peppercorns

Preheat the oven to 200°C/400°F/Gas mark 6. Put the bones in a roasting tin (pan) and roast for 20–30 minutes until lightly browned. (If you're using a chicken carcass and bones that you've saved from a roast, there's no need to brown them first). Tip into a saucepan in which the bones fit quite snugly. Add any other chicken trimmings and the remaining ingredients.

Add just enough water to cover the bones and bring slowly to the boil. Reduce the heat to its lowest setting and cook, uncovered, for about 2 hours. Make sure the stock isn't bubbling furiously – the liquid should be barely moving.

Strain the stock through a sieve into a bowl and leave to cool. Chill for up to 3 days before use. Alternatively, freeze in measured amounts, in rigid containers or sturdy freezer bags.

beef stock

Make beef stock from bones you've acquired from the butcher, or leftover bones from a large joint. Scraggy bits of meat trimmings or the meat from a cheap cut can be added to boost flavour. Once made, stock can be reduced by boiling it down in a pan once strained. This is useful for freezing in more convenient volumes and is great for perking up soups, stews, gravy and any dishes that might be a bit thin on flavour. Use the same recipe for lamb and pork stock, substituting the appropriate bones.

Makes about 1 litre (1¾ pints)

about 1.5 kg (3 lb 5 oz) beef bones

2 large onions, unpeeled and quartered

2 large carrots, roughly chopped

2 celery sticks, roughly chopped

several bay leaves, thyme and parsley sprigs

1 tablespoon black peppercorns

Preheat the oven to 200°C/400°F/Gas mark 6. Put the bones in a roasting tin (pan) and roast for 30–40 minutes until golden. Pour off the excess fat and tip the bones into a large saucepan or stock pot.

Add the remaining ingredients and just cover with cold water. Bring slowly to the boil, reduce the heat to its lowest setting and cook, uncovered, for about 4 hours. Make sure the stock doesn't bubble furiously – the liquid should be barely shuddering.

Lift out any large pieces of bone and discard them. Strain the stock through a sieve into a bowl and leave to cool.

Chill for up to a week before use. Alternatively, freeze in measured amounts, in rigid containers or sturdy freezer bags.

apple sauce

Tangy, buttery and with just a hint of cloves, apple sauce is perfect for cutting through the fattiness of roast pork. It's also good with game and duck, and leftovers can be used in toasted baguettes with cold pork and watercress.

Serves 6

85 g (3 oz) unsalted butter

3 large cooking apples, peeled, cored and chopped

25 g (1 oz) caster (superfine) sugar

good pinch of ground cloves

finely grated zest and juice of 1 lemon

Melt 50 g (2 oz) of the butter in a saucepan. Add the apples, sugar, cloves and lemon juice and reduce the heat to its lowest setting. Cook gently, covered with a lid until the apples are very tender. Stir the apples frequently so they cook evenly.

Beat with a wooden spoon to mix the apples to a purée. Remove from the heat, dot with the remaining butter and beat in. Transfer to a serving dish and serve warm or cold.

fresh mint sauce

This is a classic accompaniment to roast lamb but also tastes great with grilled or barbecued lamb, sausages and duck breasts. Once you've made your own you'll find there is no comparison and you won't be tempted to buy ready made again.

Serves 6

25 g (1 oz) fresh garden mint, finely chopped
2 tablespoons caster (superfine) sugar

60 ml (4 tablespoons) white wine vinegar

Pull the mint leaves from the stalks and finely chop. Put in a small bowl and add the sugar and 2 tablespoon boiling water. Leave until the sugar dissolves.

Stir in the vinegar and transfer to a small serving dish.

mayonnaise

Next time you have a barbecue, or make your own burgers, try some homemade mayonnaise. It's so delicious and easy and keeps well in the refrigerator for a week. Occasionally, mayonnaise will separate because the oil has been added too quickly. If this happens pour the separated mixture into a bowl and place another egg yolk in the processor. Gradually pour in the separated mixture, which will emulsify as its combined with the egg yolk

Makes 300ml (½ pint)

2 organic egg yolks

½ teaspoon Dijon mustard

salt and freshly ground black pepper

120ml (4fl oz) mild olive oil

120ml (4fl oz) vegetable oil

15–30 ml (1–2 tablespoons) white wine vinegar

Put the egg yolks, mustard and a little seasoning into a food processor or blender and blend briefly to mix.

Combine the oils in a jug. With the machine running, gradually pour in the oil in as thin a stream as possible. The mayonnaise will gradually start to thicken. Continue adding the oil until the consistency is thick and smooth.

Blend in a tablespoon of the vinegar. Check the flavour, adding more vinegar for extra tang as well as a little extra seasoning in needed.

Variation
For a quick and easy version of a classic Aioli, finely crush one plump garlic clove and add with the egg yolks and mustard to the above mayonnaise recipe.

tomato ketchup

Impress family or friends with your homemade ketchup – it'll go down a treat, particularly with burgers, barbecues and grills.

Makes about 225ml (7 ½ fl oz)

750g (1lb 10oz) ripe tomatoes, roughly chopped

1 onion, chopped

1 garlic clove, chopped

65g (2 ½ oz) light muscovado (brown) sugar

1 tsp ground paprika

½ tsp salt

75ml (5 tbsp) red wine vinegar

Put the tomatoes, onion, garlic, sugar, paprika, salt and vinegar in a saucepan and bring to the boil. Cover with a lid and cook for 10 minutes.

Remove the lid and continue to cook the sauce for about 25 minutes, stirring frequently, until thickened and pulpy. Press through a sieve into a clean saucepan, extracting as much pulp as possible by forcing the mixture through with the back of a dessertspoon. Cook until the sauce has a consistency that thickly coats the back of a spoon. Pour into thoroughly cleaned bottles or jars. Cover and leave to cool. Chill.

mashed potatoes

Serve mashed potatoes when you are cooking a meaty stew, casserole or pot roast and don't want any delicious juices left on the plates. If you are entertaining and don't want all the cooking left until the last minute, make the mash an hour or two in advance and heat through, stirring frequently to make sure it doesn't stick on the bottom of the pan.

Serves 4

1 kg (2 lb 4 oz) small floury potatoes
salt and freshly ground black pepper

100 ml (3½ fl oz) milk or single (light) cream
25 g (1 oz) butter

Put the unpeeled potatoes in a saucepan. Cover with water and bring to the boil. Reduce the heat to a gentle simmer and cook for about 15–20 minutes until the potatoes are tender. Drain and when cool enough to handle, peel away the skins.

Return to the pan. Heat the milk or cream in a separate small saucepan until hot. Add a little to the potatoes and mash well, gradually adding the remainder. Dot the butter into the pan and beat. Season to taste with salt and pepper.

Variation

For celeriac or parsnip mash, substitute 500 g (1 lb 2 oz) celeriac or parsnips, cut into small chunks. Cook in a separate pan of water until just tender before mashing with the potatoes.

perfect roast potatoes

Use floury potatoes for roasting – they'll provide the perfect texture for a crispy crust and fluffy centre. If you're roasting them at the same time as a joint of meat, cook them on the top shelf of the oven (with the meat below) and the temperature at which the meat is roasting. Turn the oven up to crisp them while the meat is resting.

Serves 4

1 kg (2 lb 4 oz) floury potatoes   vegetable oil, mild olive oil, beef dripping,
salt   duck or goose fat

Preheat the oven to 220°C/425°F/Gas mark 7. Peel and cut the potatoes into chunky pieces. Bring a saucepan of salted water to the boil, add the potatoes and cook for 5 minutes to soften. Drain through a colander. Once dry, shake the potatoes around in the colander until their surfaces are roughed up a bit.

Heat a thin layer of oil or fat in a roasting tin (pan) on the stove top. Tip in the potatoes and turn them in the fat. Roast for about 1 hour, turning the potatoes two or three times so they develop an even crust.

creamy polenta

This is another great accompaniment, ideal for soaking up meaty juices. It's great with rich Italian stews and tomato-based sauces. Spoon onto serving plates or dishes before piling the meat and juices on top.
Serves 4

250 g (9 oz) polenta

75 ml (5 tablespoons) olive oil or 50 g (2 oz) butter

salt and freshly ground black pepper

Bring 1 litre (1¾ pints) water to the boil in a large saucepan. Once bubbling away, slowly tip in the polenta in a thin, steady stream, stirring continuously with a wooden spoon as you do so.

Once all the polenta is added, continue to stir the mixture over a low heat until it is very thick and bubbles occasionally rise from the base of the pan. Beat in the olive oil or butter and a little seasoning to taste.

COUSCOUS

Couscous is really good with spicy dishes, particularly North African and Middle Eastern inspired ones. It's also so easy to make. Leftovers can be transformed into a simple salad by stirring in roasted vegetables, nuts or seeds and chopped herbs.

Serves 5–6

350 g (12 oz) couscous
2 teaspoons vegetable bouillon powder or
   ½ vegetable stock cube

25 g (1 oz) butter or 30 ml (2 tablespoons) olive oil
salt and freshly ground black pepper

Tip the couscous into a large heatproof bowl. Add the bouillon powder or stock cube to 400 ml (14 fl oz) boiling water in a jug. Stir to dissolve and pour over the couscous. Cover with foil and leave to stand for 10 minutes.

Use a fork to stir the couscous and separate the grains. Dot with the butter or drizzle with oil and add a little salt and pepper to taste. Stir together and pile into a warmed serving dish.

butter shortcrust pastry

This variation on classic shortcrust pastry gives a lovely buttery flavour and a light, slightly flaky texture that's so good with meat dishes – or any other! There's also no 'rubbing in' so it's very easy to make.

Makes 450 g (1 lb)

250 g (9 oz) plain (all-purpose) flour, plus
  extra for dusting
150 g (5 oz) firm lightly salted butter

2 medium egg yolks
about 90 ml (6 tablespoons) ice cold water

Put the flour in a bowl. Coarsely grate the butter directly over the flour, stopping and stirring the butter into the flour as you go so it doesn't cake together in one lump. Add the egg yolks and water and mix with a round bladed knife until the ingredients start to form a dough. Once the dough is caking together use your hands to form it into a paste. If the dough feels dry and crumbly, add a dash more water but do this gradually as too much water will make the dough soggy.

Turn out onto the surface and lightly knead the dough together into a smooth ball. Wrap and chill for at least 30 minutes before using.

INDEX

About the author

Joanna Farrow is a food writer and stylist with thirty years experience, initially on women's magazines and then freelance, continuing to work for a variety of food and women's magazines. She has
also written cookbooks on a diverse range of subjects including meat, fish, preserves, ice-cream,
chocolate, baking and kids cooking. Since moving to a rural environment Joanna has developed a
passion for gardening and has become absorbed in her hugely satisfying herb garden. She also en-
joys travelling and seeking out new culinary ideas to add a creative twist to recipe writing.

First published in 2012 by New Holland Publishers (UK) Ltd
London • Cape Town • Sydney • Auckland
www.newhollandpublishers.com

Garfield House 86–88 Edgware Road London W2 2EA, UK
Wembley Square Solan Street, Gardens Cape Town 8000 South Africa
Unit 1, 66 Gibbes Street Chatswood New South Wales 2067 Australia
218 Lake Road Northcote Auckland New Zealand

Special thanks to speciality butcher Springbok Delights in Lane Cove for their support, Jeremy Hicks, Adam Mc Conville
and Reon Wisenach.

ISBN 978 1 84773 999 5

Publisher: Clare Sayer
Publishing Director: Lliane Clarke
Project Editor: Simona Hill
Designer: Tracy Loughlin
Photographer: Tony Briscoe and Graeme Gillies
Cover photograph: Graeme Gillies/NHIL
Senior Production Coordinator: Marion Storz
Printer: Toppan Leefung Printing Ltd

10 9 8 7 6 5 4 3 2 1